D1715640

ANTISLAVERY DISCOURSE AND NINETEENTH-CENTURY AMERICAN LITERATURE

Also by Julie Husband (and Jim O'Loughlin):

DAILY LIFE IN THE INDUSTRIAL UNITED STATES: 1870–1900

ANTISLAVERY DISCOURSE AND NINETEENTH-CENTURY AMERICAN LITERATURE

INCENDIARY PICTURES

Julie Husband

ANTISLAVERY DISCOURSE AND NINETEENTH-CENTURY AMERICAN LITERATURE
Copyright © Julie Husband, 2010

First published in 2010 by PALGRAVE MACMILLAN® in the
United States - a division of St. Martin's Press LLC, 175 Fifth Avenue,
New York, NY 10010.

Where this book is distributed in the UK, Europe and the rest of the
World, this is by Palgrave Macmillan, a division of Macmillan
Publishers Limited, registered in England, company number 785998,
of Houndmills, Basingstoke, Hampshire RG21 6XS.

Palgrave Macmillan is the global academic imprint of the above
companies and has companies and representatives throughout the world.

Palgrave® and Macmillan® are registered trademarks in the United
States, the United Kingdom, Europe and other countries.

ISBN: 978–0–230–62148–0

Library of Congress Cataloging-in-Publication Data
Husband, Julie.
    Antislavery discourse and nineteenth-century American literature :
    incendiary pictures / Julie Husband.
        p.   cm.
    ISBN 978–0–230–62148–0 (alk. paper)
    1. Antislavery movements—United States—History—19th century.
    2. Abolitionists—United States—History—19th century.   3. Women
    abolitionists—United States—History—19th century.   4. Social
    reformers—United States—History—19th century.   5. Slavery in
    literature.   6. Protest literature, American—History and criticism.
    7. Labor—United States—History—19th century.
    8. Industrialization—United States—Social aspects—History—
    19th century.   9. Working class—United States—Social conditions—
    History—19th century.   I. Title.
    E449.H97 2010
    326′.80973—dc22   2009023185

Design by Integra Software Services

First edition: February 2010

10 9 8 7 6 5 4 3 2 1

Printed in the United States of America

For Jim O'Loughlin

PERMISSIONS

Publication of this book was supported by grants from the College of Humanities and Fine Arts and the Graduate College of the University of Northern Iowa.

I gratefully acknowledge permission to publish the following:

An earlier version of Chapter 2 was published as "Anticipating Progressive Era Reformers: Lydia Maria Child and the Mothering State," *ESQ: A Journal of the American Renaissance* 50.4 (Spring 2006): 283–314. Copyright 2006 by the Board of Regents of Washington State University.

An earlier version of Chapter 5 was published as "'The White Slave of the North:' Lowell Mill Women and the Reproduction of 'Free' Labor," *Legacy: A Journal of Nineteenth-Century American Women Writers* 16.1 (May 1999): 11–21. Reprinted from *Legacy: A Journal of American Women Writers* by permission of the University of Nebraska Press. ⓒ 1999.

"Who Bids? Incendiary Pictures" was printed on the last page of the *Anti-Slavery Record* of August 1836. Courtesy of Special Collections, University of Virginia Library.

CONTENTS

PREFACE

As I am writing I am drinking coffee from a mug my brother-in-law gave us. When it heats up the map printed on it shows the effects of rising tide levels caused by global warming. The mug is a gimmick, and yet I cannot help but notice that Florida is wiped out by rising tides. And I am reminded every day of this threat when I have my cup of coffee.

This daily practice reminds me of the inventive ways in which mid-nineteenth-century abolitionists made the issue of Southern slavery an immediate concern to Northerners who were themselves struggling with the changes wrought by industrialization. They organized a host of activities—petition campaigns, traveling lecturers, antislavery bazaars, antislavery singing troupes, sugar boycotts, and, most importantly, pro-duction and sale of antislavery commodities—to fund antislavery efforts. All of these encouraged conversion to antislavery by making it more than a political position: abolitionists made it a culture, a whole way of life that drew in many from the dominant culture and succeeded in associating slavery with sin even for those who resisted antislavery activism.

I never cease to be amazed by the persistence and resourcefulness of the relatively small band of committed radicals who braved censure and violence to spread their message. This book examines one of the key ingre-dients of their success: their ability to impact the "common sense" logic of the dominant culture, a common sense that told Americans that slavery was profitable, that slaveowners could be trusted with extraordinary power over their slaves, and that African Americans were better off as slaves than wage workers. Because of my focus on the interplay of radical ideas and popular culture, I examine texts and performances that had either a wide circulation—in the cases of "Letters from New York," *The Hidden Hand*, and Frederick Douglass's speeches—or demonstrated a pattern of think-ing among the key constituency of downwardly mobile, white, middle class people—in the case of *The Scarlet Letter* and the *Lowell Offering*. Each of these works moved from representations of slavery to comparative representations of free labor society, showing how this campaign differentiated between the two systems and impacted perceptions of the emerging wage labor system in America.

ACKNOWLEDGMENTS

I want to thank my colleagues who read and commented upon portions of this book and whose suggestions and encouragement were invaluable—especially Wally Hettle, Jeremy Schraffenberger, and participants in Samuel Gladden's "Usual Third" research collective at the University of Northern Iowa. Jim Trotman of West Chester University, a friend and mentor, offered key suggestions on the Frederick Douglass and *Lowell Offering* chapters. I sincerely appreciate the financial support of David Walker of the Graduate College, Reinhold Bubser of the College of Humanities and Fine Arts, and Jeffrey Copeland of the Department of English. In a prior incarnation, this book benefitted from the close reading and inspiring discussions I had with my dissertation committee—Neil Schmitz, Stacy Hubbard, and Bill Fischer. The editorial suggestions of Jana Argersinger and Albert J. von Frank (*ESQ*) and of Jean Pfaelzer and Sharon M. Harris (*Legacy*) challenged me to test and develop my argument and have impacted the entirety of this book. Many thanks to my parents, Bert and Kathleen Husband, and my in-laws, Jim and Joan O'Loughlin, who love me even when I'm distracted and to my children, Nic, Devin, and Ian O'Loughlin, who provide such wonderful opportunities for distraction. The richness they bring to my life is the best inspiration. And to my first and best reader, Jim O'Loughlin, thank you for giving me the hard advice, the right term, the next book to read, the pep talk, and the clear-your-head run.

INTRODUCTION

When Harriet Beecher Stowe said in 1853 that "the worst abuse of the system of slavery is its outrage upon the family," she was tapping into an increasingly popular strain of antislavery argument (*Key* 133). In the mid-1830s, abolitionists launched an explosive "family protection" campaign, publicizing the destruction of slave families in the slave market, the vulnerability of slave women to sexual exploitation, and the spectacle of white masters selling their own children. Despite accusations that their campaign catered to prurient tastes, abolitionists, especially women, eventually succeeded in connecting slavery, sexual exploitation, and the separation of families in the public mind. Their campaign prepared the public to receive Stowe's best-selling novel, *Uncle Tom's Cabin*, which was to codify American perceptions of slavery for the next century. Comparing the reception of *Uncle Tom's Cabin* with that of the 1835 antislavery novel *Archy Moore*, abolitionist Wendell Phillips said the earlier novel "owed its want of success to no lack of genius, but only to the fact that it was a work born out of due time" (131). Phillips argued that between 1835 and 1852, the abolitionists "broke up the crust of an ignorant prejudice [and] roused a slumbering conscience" using "the very tools by which [public opinion] was formed" (109–10). In other words, they tapped into emerging trends in literature—sentimental literature, most especially—to encourage identification with slaves' suffering and to rouse humanitarian action.

The American women's rights movement emerged from abolition for several reasons.[1] Its primary organizers—women such as the Grimke sisters, Sojourner Truth, Frances Ellen Watkins Harper, Elizabeth Cady Stanton, Susan B. Anthony, Lucy Stone, and Lucretia Mott—received their first training in organizational politics through the antislavery movement. It also helped them to free themselves from the social taboos and institutions that inhibited women from speaking or writing about public issues. Antislavery activism, much like the revivals of the Second Great Awakening, allowed women to defy, in the name of God and morality, a conservative, institutionally protected clergy.[2] Questioning the authority of the clergy regarding slavery, they soon learned to question its authority over women's social roles.[3] Moreover, they saw their own condition in marriage as akin to that of the slave, prohibited in marriage from the ability to form contracts, hold property, control their wages, or control their sexuality. Women's stories about slavery and their marketing network finally rendered the slave South a morally bankrupt society in the minds of many Northerners. The abolitionists' family protection campaign used images and narratives drawn from women's experiences in slavery, told from women's perspectives, and appealing, frequently, to women. It was this family protection campaign, rather than prior antislavery efforts, that captured the attention and sympathy of a critical number of Americans.

Recent scholarship has argued that white antislavery feminists sometimes appropriated the stories of female slaves to advance their own interests, sometimes at the expense of black women. As Karen Sanchez–Eppler argues, "The difficulty of preventing moments of identification from becoming acts of appropriation constitutes the essential dilemma of feminist-abolitionist rhetoric" (20). It is my contention that economic changes in the 1830s, 1840s, and 1850s caused unprecedented intrusions of the marketplace into family life for Northerners of all classes and for slave families in the South, promoting a very real sense of common cause among white and black women. In the chapters that follow, I examine the power of antislavery sentimentality to reshape the role of women in industrial society and to foster politically vital coalitions, while still noting those moments when identification failed and white women used the language of antislavery to pursue separate and even hostile ends.

The fiction, poetry, woodcuts, and dramatic speeches of abolitionists sold through an extensive network of antislavery societies succeeded in changing the "common sense" understanding of family in antebellum America.[4] The incendiary pictures of slave families distributed by the antislavery movement not only changed public opinion about slavery but became powerful vehicles for working-class and feminist movements as well. This book examines how these antislavery stories shaped the way labor leaders and early feminists depicted and sought to reform "free society" in the North.

ABOLITION, INDUSTRIALISM, AND DOMESTICITY: CHALLENGES TO AMERICAN REPUBLICAN RHETORIC

Three great social upheavals challenged the stories Americans told about themselves during the antebellum period, provoking new narratives and figures for describing American-ness and for condemning the anti-American nature of, above all, slavery. Out of the pressures of industrial capitalism, evangelical abolition, and the privatization of the family grew the family protection campaign of the abolitionists. This counter-hegemonic campaign, in turn, shaped the ways in which Americans experienced structural changes.[5] Ultimately, the family protection campaign influenced the direction and pace of these structural shifts.

Emerging industrial capitalism in the North produced large numbers of impoverished, marginally employed workers. By 1860, wage earners accounted for 40 percent of the U.S. labor force, up from only 12 percent in 1800 (Lebergott 290–1). For a country founded upon the Republican ideal of the independent citizen—the yeomen farmer—this shift in population forced a reexamination of what it meant to be free and independent. Americans anxiously discussed the "Social Question," looking for an alternative to the perceived degradation and unrest of England's industrial wage workers. Amy Dru Stanley argues that with this rise in wage-dependent workers, Americans had to "distinguish between what was saleable and what was not" (ix). By implication, in the nineteenth century, which legal scholars have termed the "age of contract," Americans had to decide who could make contracts and who could not, establishing "the moral boundaries of market relations" (xi). Stanley goes on to argue that the ability to enter into contracts, as opposed to the ownership of capital, increasingly came to define freedom. As a result, both slavery and marriage became the subject of controversy. Redefining the wage laborer as "free" because of his ability to make contracts, called into question the justice of the slave's and wife's inability to form contracts.

Both because of this distinction between wage worker and slave and because of deteriorating wages and work conditions, many in the working class felt both an identification with the slave and a strong compulsion to distinguish themselves from the slave.[6] Contrary to the way abolitionism is often portrayed, antislavery societies were primarily composed of working-class and lower-middle-class people,[7] drawn to the movement, in part, because they saw in the slave's exploitation a parallel to their own. Antislavery agitation gave a vocabulary and an iconography to the emerging working-class movements.

Industrial development not only expanded the numbers of wage-dependent workers, but it also led to the expansion of slavery. Textile mills in the North and in Britain demanded more and more cotton. Soil exhaustion in the Old South, Indian removal in the Deep South, rising cotton prices, and technological innovation all contributed to a shift in population from the Old South (the coastal states from Georgia to Virginia) toward the rich lands of the Deep South (Louisiana, Mississippi, Alabama, and inland Georgia) (Gutman 183–219). With the legal end to the international slave trade, slaves became a valuable export for the Old South. The internal slave trade was small and localized prior to 1790, but it exploded after 1790. One million African American slaves were sold from the Old South to the New South between 1790 and 1860, and two million were sold locally (Deyle 4). Nearly one-third of slave families were separated between 1820 and 1860, and this breakup of families became one of the distinctive features of American slavery (Oakes 9).[8] No other slave society separated husbands and wives or parents and children on this scale.

The second midcentury development to impact antislavery discourse was the rise of evangelical abolition, which drew upon the following trends for its emotional fervor: this separation of slave families, the discontent of working-class Northerners, and the antiestablishment revivalism of the Second Great Awakening. Beginning with William Lloyd Garrison's 1832 frontal attack on the American Colonization Society, Garrisonian abolitionists demanded the immediate and uncompensated emancipation of all American slaves. Unlike their British antislavery counterparts, the Garrisonians challenged the property rights of a powerful group of citizens and attacked the social organization of a large section of their country. Slave labor was enormously profitable—Seymour Drescher has referred to the campaign to end the slave trade as "econocide," and the same should be said of the American antislavery campaign. It was a truly revolutionary movement that aimed to persuade Americans to destroy a prolific part of their economy. To do this, abolitionists had to challenge the hegemonic or "common sense" understanding of slavery as a benevolent, or at least necessary, institution. And unlike their American predecessors, the Garrisonian abolitionists believed in agitation; all Americans were implicated in the sin of slavery so long as the Constitution recognized property rights in people. Theirs was both an evangelical and revolutionary movement. It focused on the culpability of Northerners in the sin of slavery and attacked the very bedrock of American narratives, the Constitution, as a proslavery, anti-freedom, hypocritical document.

The third midcentury transition occurred inside the Northern family. With the shift of production outside of the home, new family and social patterns emerged.[9] The burgeoning domestic discourse, sometimes called sentimentality, drew a firm distinction between the public world of men, in which the capitalist ethos of competition and individualism prevailed, and the private world of women, in which the domestic ethos of cooperation between strong and weak, young and old prevailed. In her study of domestic fiction, Nina Baym locates the height of the genre between 1820 and 1870 when novels "by American women authors about women" dominated the literary marketplace (*Woman's Fiction* 11). Baym argues that women used domestic discourse to assert the superiority of their alternative values and carve out an elevated social function for themselves. "The domestic ideal," Baym writes, "meant not that woman was to be sequestered from the world in her place at home but that everybody was to be placed in the home and hence home and the world would become one" (27).

A more conservative manifestation of domestic discourse, sentimentality described women's nature as other-centered and prescribed a selflessness for them. As a result, much sentimental discourse revealed women to exert power through identification with the suffering of others and through their own personal suffering. This understanding of women's nature—and romantic racialism extended this characterization to African American men and women—led to a masochistic form of power that could prove problematic for both women's and African Americans' empowerment.[10]

A more progressive form of domestic discourse was inextricably linked to the development of the quasi-public sphere of the "social." In its early phase, it claimed that women's expertise in managing the household and disciplining children fitted them perfectly for the emerging "helping" professions—social work, medical care, and education. These helping professions, in turn, were made possible by the economic surplus of industrial capitalism and made necessary by the fear of social instability that industrialism provoked.

Both the core of the antislavery movement—leading speakers and writers like Lydia Maria Child, David Child, Henry Clarke Wright, Stephen Foster, and Abby Kelley—and many of those who articulated the cult of domesticity were drawn from the lower-middle classes. As the sons and daughters of small shopkeepers, small farmers, and independent craftsmen, these men and women, Stephanie Coontz argues, "had the most to gain and to lose in the transformation of the artisan republic; women were central to how successfully families negotiated the challenge" (186). In their ambivalence toward the emerging economic order, the writers I discuss in the succeeding chapters use the family protection campaign to produce a range of ideological effects. At the heart of both domestic fiction and the family protection campaign are moments of sentimental identification, when bodily suffering, tears, or the loss of a loved one provide transcendent moments of understanding across dramatically different race, gender, and class experiences. In the following chapters, I investigate the intersection between domestic discourse, the rise of a mass antislavery movement, and ongoing concerns about first-wave industrialization in the United States.

This book is divided into two sections. The first examines several of the most influential women propagandists in the movement: the women who collectively organized the major antislavery fund-raisers and produced *The Liberty Bell*, a gift book designed to raise money as well as awareness, and Lydia Maria Child, arguably the most prolific and inventive antislavery writer in America. The second section investigates writers who adapted the antislavery family protection campaign to theorize and advocate for other groups: Nathaniel Hawthorne for the downwardly mobile in early industrial capitalism; E.D.E.N. Southworth for Southern, white women; and the writers of the *Lowell Offering* for white, working-class women.

I begin by describing the emergence of the family protection campaign and its fundamental break with prior antislavery campaigns in leadership, strategy, and message. Women provided the financial leadership, hosting the major fund-raisers and writing the most emotionally resonant stories, sold in gift books. These gift books, along with the other antislavery products available at major fairs, promoted an everyday practice of antislavery activism, turning a debate topic into a way of life.

The next chapter examines Lydia Maria Child, one of the most successful propagandists of the antislavery movement. She converted many to the movement with her sensational depictions of tragic mulattas, but even as she was developing this trope as a shorthand for the injustices of slavery, she was popularizing another trope to illustrate the dangers of industrialization. The Northern street urchin appears repeatedly in her popular, though critically neglected, column "Letters from New York." This precariously free child exposed the dangers of Northern individualism. Comparing these two figures shows how Child's antislavery agitation influenced her views of emerging industrial capitalism. She used both in the early 1840s when she was editor of the *National Antislavery Standard* and living in New York City. The "Letters" recorded her impressions of major New York institutions, neighborhoods, and cultural destinations and offered Child the opportunity to study the most industrialized city in the United States. She developed a sometimes penetrating and sometimes conflicted analysis of class, race, and gender in the new urban landscape. The street child, a recurrent figure throughout the column, represented the failures and excessive freedom of the market economy, failures Child sought to address through her theory of the "mothering state."

My third chapter examines Nathaniel Hawthorne's *The Scarlet Letter*, a novel that many have suggested was animated by his attraction and repulsion toward feminism, abolitionism, and the two women in his life who most directly embodied these movements: Margaret Fuller and his sister-in-law, Elizabeth Peabody. Hester, the scarlet woman who is nearly branded for her antinomian beliefs, seeks to renegotiate the meaning of her sign by circulating in the Puritan marketplace. Like the feminist abolitionists who broke taboos by marketing essays, gift books, and samplers decrying the sexual abuse of slave women, Hester converts her stigma into a sign of distinction and circulates in the marketplace as a technique for redefining the significance of her scarlet letter. While intellectually resistant to the antislavery movement, Hawthorne was powerfully swayed by it emotionally, suggesting the latent potential of the family protection campaign to convert even conservative individuals.

Like Lydia Maria Child, E.D.E.N. Southworth frequently wrote of tragic mulattas and the color line, and she saw the Northern street urchin as emblematic of Northern labor relations.[11] However, in her most popular novel, *The Hidden Hand, or Capitola the Mad-Cap*, Southworth imagines the Northern street urchin as far more resilient than Child did. Capitola, a cross-dressing tomboy raised in New York City, ultimately avenges Southern white women, who are portrayed as the primary victims of slave society. Southworth's comic romp amounts to a sustained critique not only of "the patriarchal institution" but also of female masochism and sentimentality. Unlike Child's work, Southworth's novels clearly do slide from "moments of identification" between free and slave women to "moments of appropriation" when the drama of the slave mistress and the agenda of white women eclipse those of slave women. Her novels, especially this one, illustrate why the coalition between the women's rights movement and African American civil rights movement collapses after the Civil War.

White, working-class women also developed an identification with slave women and used the family protection campaign to represent themselves and to imagine ways of resolving oppression within the family or the workplace. The *Lowell Offering*, written and edited by female operatives at the Lowell mills in Massachusetts, uses many of the same plot devices and tropes prevalent in antislavery fiction. Contemporary critics have derided the *Lowell Offering* as having insufficient working-class consciousness; yet, the female-edited paper was intensely interested in the intersection between the household and workplace politics. In the family dramas of the *Lowell Offering*, class relations are overlaid by family relations, as the stories of runaway domestics indicate. The famous "mill girls" of Lowell, Massachusetts, adopted slave narratives in surprising ways to figure farm life, rather than factory life, as more exploitative and sexually threatening. Even as working-class women were figured as "white slaves of the North" by male labor leaders, they joined antislavery movements and defined themselves in contrast to slave women. Factory work was often figured as an alternative to their subordination within farm families. Far from being "white slaves of the North," they found in industrial labor a way to escape the fate of the farm wife, a fate they figured as enslavement. Antislavery imagery and narratives provided a means to express a coded critique of the seemingly pastoral life of the farm wife.

The antislavery family protection campaign used familial narratives to challenge the common sense of the nation. All of the writers discussed here struggled with contradictory American narratives and invented new ways for imagining the story of America. These inventions opened up possibilities for accommodating changes the authors could not control. Thanks to the writers of *The Liberty Bell*, Hawthorne, and Southworth, it became possible to imagine women exerting pressure in the public realm through market circulation, not in the compromised form of the prostitute, but in the emerging form of the social and cultural worker. Thanks to Child, it became possible to imagine a social safety net operating outside parish communities to meet the instability of industrial capitalism. Thanks to the writers of the *Lowell Offering*, it became possible to imagine the family farm, the sine qua non of American independence, as a kind of slavery for women and wage work as an alternative.

In my final chapter, I argue that the Civil War and the emancipation of slaves demanded a new set of tropes and narratives for the empowerment of African Americans. Focusing on abolitionist Frederick Douglass, I show that after the Civil War he largely rejected the abolitionist discourses he had drawn upon in his first two autobiographies and as an antislavery leader. He adopted new tropes to make the case for African American voting and civil rights. Douglass's post–Civil War speeches show how he struggled to articulate an African American masculinity that placed African Americans within the larger American family without falling into the masochistic role so often assigned to them in antislavery sentimentality. The post–Civil War speeches show Douglass as a performer taking on a variety of personas and drawing attention to his own body as representative of the new biracial nation. They balance humor with righteous indignation and satire with denunciation, to break through to resistant white listeners while fostering an image of unbowed masculinity at odds with the martyred figures and broken families featured so prominently in the antislavery campaign. He replaces these figures with the Civil War soldier, the craftsman, and the yeomen farmer, and he adapts free labor and free market philosophies to the needs of freed slaves. These amazing performances change our perception of Douglass from the lionized larger-than-life figure portrayed in recent criticism to a far more variable, playful, daring speaker. His performances drew enormous crowds, and newspaper articles of the day suggest that he tested and sometimes crossed the boundaries of acceptable public speech and performance. Douglass's rhetoric marks a decisive shift in the campaign for black liberation and a final commentary on the possibilities and limitations of antislavery sentimentality.

PART 1

CENTRAL FEMINIST ABOLITIONISTS AND THE WAGE LABOR SYSTEM

CHAPTER 1

THE EMERGENCE OF THE FAMILY PROTECTION CAMPAIGN AND ANTISLAVERY SENTIMENTALITY

He that Stealeth a Man and Selleth him, or if he be found in his hand, he shall surely be put to Death.

Exodus 21:16, Quoted by Samuel Sewall
in *The Selling of Joseph* (1700)

I know of no law, but one which I am not at liberty to argue before this Court, no law, statute or constitution, no code, no treaty, applicable to the proceedings of the Executive or the Judiciary, except that law (pointing to the copy of the Declaration of Independence, hanging against one of the pillars of the court-room), that law, two copies of which are ever before the eyes of your Honors. I know of no other law that reaches the case of my clients, but the law of Nature and of Nature's God on which our fathers placed our own national existence.

John Quincy Adams in his 1840 court defense
of the African captives turned rebels aboard the *Amistad*.
Printed in *The Amistad Case* (1840)

She is weeping, bitterly weeping,
Far away in the tangled wild;
And in her arms, all sweetly sleeping,
Is clasped a fair young child . . .

But the father of that babe,
Which hath his azure eye
And his sunny hair, hath he betrayed
And left them there to die?

No! that were far more kind;
But it is not even so!
With his hunting train he is close behind;
She hath heard their loud hollo . . .
                    Martha Hempstead, "The Fugitive"
                         from *The Liberty Bell* (1845)

Until American women took on a leadership role in antislavery activism
in the 1830s, antislavery appeals had generally taken two forms: biblical interpretation and Enlightenment references to the slave's natural
rights. The Bible, the Declaration of Independence, and the Constitution were authoritative documents nonconformists could draw upon to
challenge the prevailing belief that slavery was, at worst, a necessary evil.
The challenge was to convince listeners that these revered documents
were inherently antislavery, and powerful arguments were developed to
deny this. Moreover, parsing these documents served to shift the focus
away from the daily lives of slaves and the suffering that slave society
imposed upon those permanently denied family, citizenship, and economic rights. Nonetheless, the shortcomings of earlier discourses serve to
highlight the strengths of the family protection campaign of the feminist
abolitionists.

One of the first Americans to become an outspoken critic of the
African slave trade was Samuel Sewall, whose 1700 pamphlet, *The Selling
of Joseph*, was structured by biblical quotes. In Sewall's central analogy, he
compared the Puritan practice of holding slaves to the betrayal of Joseph
in Genesis. Joseph's brothers sell him into slavery because they are jealous of the boy, who is his father's favorite. The only point of comparison
Sewall drew upon was the relationship between enslaver and enslaved. For
Sewall, the slave's right to freedom derived from his brotherly relationship to the colonist; as children of God neither had the right to enslave
the other. Sewall, unlike the "family protection" writers of the antebellum period, stressed the lateral relation of brother to brother, a masculine
paradigm continued in the natural rights arguments.

Sewall, like others after him, did not argue that domestic slavery or the
slave trade should be illegal, but that colonists should reject it on ethical
and practical grounds. In 1700, when Sewall wrote *The Selling of Joseph*,
slavery was considered primarily an ethical rather than a legal matter.
While the issue was debated in public, even the most organized antislavery elements, the Quakers, pursued an individual and ethical, rather

than judicial or legislative, method of stemming slavery. The Quaker Antislavery International, as David Brion Davis has termed it, approached antislavery activism as missionary work.[1] Convinced that God would punish slaveholders for their sin of "man stealing," they tried to persuade slaveholding Quakers to use free rather than slave labor.

Natural rights theory, according to which each person, regardless of the terms of any particular social contract, should be able to dispose of his or her body and labor as he or she chooses, reframed slavery as a political issue. As historian Larry Tise argues, "Natural rights theory posed the first major challenge to proslavery thought in America" (24). Because natural rights formed the cornerstone of the Declaration of Independence and the ideology of the American Revolution, it stimulated discussions of gradual abolition throughout the United States in the early national period, even in the Virginia legislature.

In an exemplary use of natural rights to attack slavery, John Quincy Adams asserted the fundamental right of men to own property in themselves in his defense of the *Amistad* Africans. Adams defended 43 kidnapped Africans who had rebelled against their Spanish captors en route to Cuba and had landed on Long Island in 1839. On Long Island, the Africans were captured by American military officers who demanded salvage, a percentage of the cargo's value, for returning the prisoners. As the Spaniards argued with the American officers over salvage, antislavery activists came to the aid of the Africans.

The complex legal case involved both international and national laws. International law protected the right to salvage for a party recovering property taken by pirates, but it also prohibited the Atlantic slave trade. Adams argued that the Africans could not be returned to their Spanish captors as salvaged property because the Spaniards had no property rights in Africans illegally kidnapped from Africa. Adams extended his argument beyond the Spaniards' violation of international law, however, to assert a natural law, enshrined in the Declaration of Independence, protecting a person's property in himself or herself. The trial became a media event with obvious implications for domestic slavery.

Eventually, Adams won the case, but only on the basis of the international law prohibiting the slave trade. The courts did not support freedom on the basis of the Africans' natural rights. Despite the victory, the case marked a decline in the power of natural rights' discourse. According to Larry Tise, nativist feelings and growing economic inequality undermined American beliefs in the fundamental equality of men. If economic inequalities, growing larger throughout the Jacksonian period, occurred naturally through the market's "invisible hand," then perhaps other forms of inequality did as well. Perhaps, according to this logic, racial and gender inequalities also occurred naturally and need not be remedied by a universal application of "natural rights." Tise notes the growth of the "positive good" thesis among defenders of slavery who increasingly challenged the Enlightenment doctrine of natural rights based upon fundamental human equality:

> The great proslavery revolution that occurred in America during the 1830's was not the development of new proslavery arguments. It was instead the general shift of Americans to a new perspective on their own society that could tolerate the perpetuation of slavery. The real revolution was a national rejection of the libertarian heritage of the American Revolution.
>
> (262)

The "self-evident" equality of men was severely challenged by the rise of nativism and the growth of a significant landless, wage-dependent community in the North.

Initially, the radical abolitionists known as "Garrisonians" returned to Sewall's use of the Bible to authorize their attack on slavery. William Lloyd Garrison pioneered a combination of religious perfectionism and anarchism that fundamentally changed the strategy and discourse of the antislavery movement. When he combined forces with two sisters from South Carolina, firsthand witnesses to slavery, they took the nation by storm. Angelina and Sarah Grimke moved North, converted to Quakerism, and broke with their family when they denounced the institution of slavery. In her 1836 "Appeal to the Christian Women of the South," Angelina Grimke combined biblical exegesis with a call for direct political action, conceived of as Christian martyrdom. She developed one of the most complex and exhaustive antislavery readings of the Bible, reiterating previous arguments that claimed black Africans were not the descendants of Ham and that Southern chattel slavery was fundamentally different from Hebrew slavery. But Grimke went beyond previous biblical readings to encourage Southern women to rebel against their social order and martyr themselves—like Christian women before them—to a holy cause. Grimke recommended that women engage in acts of civil disobedience by teaching slaves to read and by freeing them, submitting to whatever legal penalties ensued. Importantly, Grimke exhorted women to agitate within their families, influencing husbands to renounce slavery and teaching slaves to become more self-reliant through reading. Lacking immediate political power, women could still exert political influence as long as they took themselves seriously as "responsible moral being[s]," itself a controversial assertion in 1837 (qtd. in Mayer 233).

Proslavery writers, however, were equally adept at using the Bible to demonstrate that slavery was divinely sanctioned. Eugene Genovese even argues that proslavery theologians could find more in the Bible supporting slavery than antislavery theologians could find to denounce it. Proslavery writers continued to appeal to the words of the Bible and the Constitution to secure slavery's moral and legal foundations long after antislavery Northerners began stressing "the spirit" of Christianity and democracy in order to condemn slavery.

According to Genovese, Southern conservatives, exemplified by Reverend James Henley Thornwell, the "Calhoun of the Church," rejected the liberal theology sweeping the North and advocated slavery as a systemic solution to the "Social Question" (*The Southern Front*). To avoid all out class warfare, stemming from the impoverishment of the industrial working classes, Thornwell and leading theologians recommended the extension of slavery's "cradle to grave security" to the white working class. By recommending reforms, Thornwell countered claims like Grimke's that chattel slavery in a market economy did not much resemble biblical slavery. He proposed legalizing slave marriages, repealing the ban on slave literacy, and punishing cruel masters. If employers became "warrantors" of their employees, Thornwell claimed, they would be personally bound to the particular needs of their wards. Slavery, in this case, could be a "positive good" that resolved the suffering and instability that marked working-class life.

As many have demonstrated, natural rights discourse was a particularly masculine discourse, theoretically defining the political subject as an abstract, disembodied citizen, which was in practice embodied by the white male.[2] If biblical exegesis and natural rights arguments were founded on the idea that all men were "brothers" and equally entitled to a degree of independence, the "family protection" campaign stressed that women and children within slavery were dependents outside the normal restraints affection imposed upon husbands and fathers. Sewall argued it was wrong to enslave Africans, "children of God," because it was wrong for the Israelites to sell their brother Joseph. Adams argued that the *Amistad* Africans—nearly all of whom were adult men—were men "created equal." The family protection campaign focused not on the equality of men across the racial divide, but on the horror of bonds of dependence without corresponding bonds of affection. It was a discourse uniquely adapted to a growing tolerance of class difference as well as the rise of domestic fiction.

Adams himself struck the first congressional family protection blow on February 27, 1837. In one of many skirmishes over the gag rule, instituted by both Northerners and Southerners to prohibit the discussion of antislavery petitions in Congress, Adams presented a petition from "Nine Ladies from Fredericksburg." It was quickly tabled, which meant, according to the gag rule, that without coming to a vote the petition would be set upon a table and never reviewed by the House or a subcommittee. Because of its Southern origin, however, Congressman John Patton, formerly of Fredericksburg, reviewed the names on the petition. Patton declared the petition not to be from ladies but from "colored" women, one of whom had "the worst fame and reputation" (qtd. in Miller 127). *The Congressional Globe* summarized Adams's reply:

> I am glad the gentleman now says he does not know these women, for if he had not disclaimed that knowledge, I might have asked who it was that made these women infamous—whether it was those of their own color or their masters. I have understood that there are those among the coloured population of slave-holding States, who bear the image of their masters.
>
> (qtd. in Miller 229)

Adams threw the House into an uproar for this unusually candid swipe at slavery in Congress. Elsewhere, however, alluding to the practice of using slave women as concubines had become a favorite tactic of feminist abolitionists. Antislavery speakers, particularly women like the Grimkes, discovered access to the political realm through exposing the danger it posed to the domestic sphere.

These women writers extended a technique pioneered by Thomas Clarkson. With his 1788 diagram of a ship inhumanely crowded with slaves, Clarkson introduced the use of shocking visuals to subvert complacency about slavery. Women writers advanced this shock approach by introducing the model observer of slavery. Frequently, in women's antislavery fiction and poetry, a firsthand observer records not only the suffering of the slave but the empathetic response of the narrator, whose identification with the slave gives evidence of her acute sensibility. Where this differs from Clarkson's slave ship is in its microscopic rather than macroscopic approach. The family protection campaign depicted the subjective experience of slavery and, unlike Clarkson's slave ship, did not objectify slaves by representing them en masse.

Beginning with the defection of Sarah and Angelina Grimke to the North and the antislavery cause, women increasingly became the inside informers on chattel slavery. Where biblical exegesis and natural rights arguments applied "universal" principles, codified in the Bible or Declaration of Independence, to the issue of slavery, women's testimonials, fiction, and poetry focused upon the personal experience of slavery. Born into a wealthy, slaveholding South Carolina family, the Grimke sisters passionately addressed audiences through their pamphlets and lectures, reaching more than 8,000 people in ten towns in just their first month of lecturing (Mayer 233). In her testimonial in *American Slavery As It Is*,

Angelina recounted her early exposure as a schoolgirl to the brutality of Southern slavery:

> I remember one day there was called into the school room to open a window, a boy whose head had been shaved in order to disgrace him, and he had been so dreadfully whipped that he could hardly walk. So horrible was the impression produced upon my mind by his heartbroken countenance and crippled person that I fainted away. The sad and ghastly countenance of one of their female mulatto slaves who used to sit on a low stool at her sewing in the piazza, is now fresh before me. She often told me, secretly, how cruelly she was whipped when they sent her to the work house. I had known so much of the terrible scourgings inflicted in that house of blood, that when I was once obliged to pass it, the very sight smote me with such horror that my limbs could hardly sustain me. I felt as if I was passing the precincts of hell.
>
> ("Testimony" 343–44)

Grimke's identification with both of these brutalized slaves makes her feel shocked and weak; yet, her responses show a type of progress she advocates for her audience. In the first case, the boy's physical presence and her identification with another child provoke her physical response. In the second case, her response is triggered not by the immediate presence of a brutalized slave, but by the recollection of a slave woman's story. Even this abstract stimulus is sufficient to produce her empathy, which she opposes to the "hardened" response of those "ruined" by their role as slaveholders. "Why I did not become totally hardened, under the daily operation of this system, God only knows; in deep solemnity and gratitude, I say, it was the *Lord's* doing, and marvelous in mine eyes" (340). Grimke's quaking response to *a recollected story* is a kind of conversion experience in which she gives evidence of her election by her superior sensibility. Her reading audience would be similarly encouraged to feel empathy as evidence of conversion.

This conversion experience threatened the clergy. The Congregational clergymen of Massachusetts collectively issued a letter in 1837 redirecting their parishioners to seek out their ministers for instruction and excoriating women reformers: "We appreciate the unostentatious prayers and efforts of women . . . in leading religious inquirers to the pastors for instruction but when she assumes the place and tone of man as public reformer . . . her character becomes unnatural" (qtd. in Mayer 234). The Grimkes accelerated their speaking schedule and drew still larger crowds.

The Garrisonian antislavery forces quickly capitalized on this new message and these messengers for recruiting converts. Women's antislavery auxiliaries had already spearheaded the petition campaigns John Quincy Adams exploited so well in Congress. Women speakers, including

Sojourner Truth, Abby Kelley, and Frances Ellen Watkins (Harper), began to offer spoken testimonials against slavery. Soon the Ladies Auxiliaries became central to the Garrisonian public relations campaign. By 1839, the women organizing the Massachusetts Antislavery Fair annually published a gift book, *The Liberty Bell*, containing sketches of slavery as well as poems and short stories exposing its cruelties.

While each issue of *The Liberty Bell* devoted some space to essays arguing for the Garrisonian brand of abolition, the heart of the gift book was composed of a cluster of closely related scenarios. Feckless slaveowners abandoned their female slave lovers and/or threatened to sell their own children; powerless female slaves fell prey to or chose death over the sexual exploitation of slaveowners; female slaveowners, in giving vent to their anger at slaves, lost all claim to being Christians or "true women"; and even the godly slaveowner found himself in debt and was forced to sell slaves, splitting up families. In each case the story was an exemplary one, standing in for countless similar episodes. In the 1845 poem "The Fugitive," it is a beautiful slave's "common fate" to be the betrayed paramour of her slavemaster and mother of his child. The slavemaster dashes her hopes that he will acknowledge their child and free both when he sends word that he has married and that she must be sold before he returns with his new bride (Hempstead 209–14). She huddles with the child clasped to her breast as her pursuers discover her.

The 1846 edition of *The Liberty Bell* contains a similar poem, "The Slave Mother." Like "The Fugitive," the poem opens with a picture of the woman holding her child, this time a female child in whom she can read her own fate.

> Her new-born child she holdeth, but feels within her heart
> It is not hers, but his who can out bid her in the mart;
> And, through the gloomy midnight, her prayer goes up on high,—
> "God grant my little helpless one in helplessness may die!"
> (Lowell 250–52)

The (white) father's denial of the child and betrayal of the woman, the threatened separation of mother and child in the "mart," and the slave-mother's desperate wish that her daughter die rather than grow up to fall victim to an owner's betrayal are all common themes of these stories.

The 1851 edition contains "Pictures of Southern Life," a sweeping catalogue of separated families; mixed-race children exploited by their father-masters; forced, loveless marriages among slaves; and "fancy slaves" of the New Orleans marketplace vying amongst one another for the most handsome and generous master (Dall 33). United in this article are the many icons deployed by the antislavery movement to destroy the image of slavery as a patriarchal structure. This series of images confronts the reader as a quasi-pornographic montage and is in some ways the model for other stories in *The Liberty Bell*. It encapsulates the basic typological characters and plots the others elaborate upon, establishing a lexicon through which stories in other newspapers, magazines, and novels can be quickly apprehended. Dall denies that her images are constructed and shaped by narrative, claiming for them a kind of cinematic vérité. "Look at them as they hang, American women, and if they were not Miracles of Nature, would you not call them Gems of Art?" (38). She claims for her images a documentary truth, an artless presence direct from nature. Subtitled "For the Drawing Rooms of American Women," the montage is meant to lodge in the everyday sight of free women. Their own commonplace domestic events would then contrast to these pictures, daily reminding them of the domestic disruptions suffered by slaves. It is the purpose of the family protection campaign in antislavery, so clearly exemplified in *The Liberty Bell*, to bind the fate of the slave as closely as possible to the everyday practices and stories of Northern family life.[3]

Making antislavery not just a political position but an everyday practice and a transformation akin to religious conversion became a goal for resourceful antislavery activists like Lydia Maria Child and many other feminist abolitionists. Child, already famous as the writer of the nation's first magazine for children, published the *Anti-Slavery Catechism* in 1835 to train children—and presumably their parents—in antislavery thinking. The catechism taught people how to respond to debates over slavery. Like Christian catechisms, it is structured by questions and answers such as the following from the beginning of the book:

Question: Why do you consider it a duty to preach and publish abolitionist doctrines?

Answer: First, I consider it my duty as a Christian; for the system of slavery, as a whole, and in each of its details, is in direct opposition to the precepts of the gospel. Secondly, I consider it my duty as a conscientious citizen of this republic; for I believe slavery is prejudicial to the best interests of my country; and I dare not hope that God's blessing will rest upon us if we persist in our iniquity. (3)

A catechism is meant to be memorized and as such must become a part of daily practices. Feminist abolitionists, because of their positions regulating the daily routines in their own homes, became expert at turning antislavery beliefs into a way of life.

While the separation of slave families had been a point of concern for earlier abolitionists, it had not been a primary focus until the Grimke sisters began their speaking and writing campaigns in the 1830s. Samuel Sewall, for example, lamented that the slave trade separated "Men from their Country, Husbands from their Wives, Parents from their Children" (11). Yet Sewall tucked this point in between warnings that slaves would increase the crime rate and predictions that they would prove unprofitable. Furthermore, Sewall never mentions the sexual exploitation of women slaves in his male-centered tract. He does allude to the "Temptations Masters are under, to connive at the Fornication of their Slaves; lest they should be obliged to find them Wives, or pay their Fines" (11). However, the integrity of white and black families in slavery was a low priority for Sewall, who was far more concerned with the prosperity of the Massachusetts Bay colony and the spiritual well-being of its white citizens.

The Grimkes and *The Liberty Bell* moved the integrity of white and black families from a marginal to a central position. The women leaders of the antislavery movement pioneered a brand of antislavery sentimentality that put human suffering, especially as signaled by weeping and other physical signs, at the center of their appeals. Theirs was a campaign that consciously critiqued the "mart" but built upon new possibilities opened up by that expanded marketplace as it became possible to encourage a humanitarian consumption of antislavery products.[4] The products available at the fairs antislavery women organized—slave narratives, gift books, sewing samplers, medallions, written music, even clothing made by women in sewing circles devoted to the cause—effectively kept the issue of slavery constantly in the minds of American families. They made the marketplace and their own roles as consumers their most potent weapons in the antislavery campaign.

ANTICIPATING PROGRESSIVE ERA REFORMERS: LYDIA MARIA CHILD AND THE MOTHERING STATE

The convergence between early nineteenth-century, emerging industrial capitalism and radical antislavery has led many to accuse abolitionists of being proponents of the increasingly widespread system of wage labor. Northern abolitionists' concern for the slave, so the logic went, was a deliberate evasion of the suffering of wage laborers closer to home. Lydia Maria Child, one of the radical abolitionists' most important leaders, serves as a case in point. Child might easily be accused of acting as an apologist for the wage labor system. She opposed the ten-hour movement and considered labor unions just as socially destructive as employer cartels. In fact, Child regarded "free labor" as an essentially moral system provided that its "worst abuses" could be curbed. Nonetheless, she was an outspoken critic of the unregulated, laissez-faire capitalism that was developing in New York in the early 1840s. Child struggled to represent industrializing New York City and to prescribe remedies for the widespread poverty, lawlessness, and social tensions she saw emanating from economic changes in the North. In her writings about Southern slavery, Child moved from essays and policy prescriptions to fictional forms that clearly supported her policies; in her treatment of Northern socioeconomic reforms, however, the two emerged together. Child's *Letters from*

New York offer a glimpse of a practiced social critic as she formed her thoughts about the new urban, industrial society and as she experimented with idioms for describing it.

In 1841 Child moved from Boston to New York to become the first female editor of an antislavery newspaper, the *National Anti-Slavery Standard*. During her nine years in New York, she traveled extensively through working-class neighborhoods and toured prisons, courts, and orphanages, institutions closely associated with the city's growing working class. The section of the *National Anti-Slavery Standard* most consistently concerned with New York's working population, and the most popular part of the paper, was her column, *Letters from New York*. Addressed to an anonymous male friend, the letters combined descriptions of New York's neighborhoods with reviews of cultural events and tourist sites. These letters, she claimed, were her opportunity to "turn wearily aside from the dusty road of reforming duty, to gather flowers in sheltered nooks, or play with gems in hidden grottoes" (*Letters from New York* 5).[1] More accurately, they became her opportunity to study the most industrialized city in the United States during the antebellum period and, under the guise of offering unedited and uneditorialized sketches, to develop a sometimes penetrating and sometimes conflicted analysis of class, race, and gender in the new urban landscape. Compared with her antislavery writings, the *Letters from New York* are more speculative and more self-conscious, as if she were experimenting with various ways of representing an entirely new experience. The tone is an inviting one that appeals to a broad audience. Indeed, when Child left the *National Anti-Slavery Standard* in 1843, the *Boston Courier* continued the series, and she published a second series in 1845.[2]

The most prevalent figure to emerge in the *Letters from New York* to represent the failures of "free labor" is the street child, a child prematurely thrust into the market economy with little parental supervision, emotional support, or social training. As Child focused on images of street children, she developed a critique of the excessive freedom of laissez-faire capitalism. She articulated a theory of the "mothering state" that guided her choice of urban reforms in the North and prefigured the maternalist politics that characterize many reform organizations in the later Progressive Era.[3]

The argument advanced here responds primarily to two long-standing debates. One concerns the relationship between antislavery agitation and capitalism. Contemporaneous proslavery writers such as journal editor James D. B. DeBow, Senator John C. Calhoun, domestic novelist Caroline Lee Hentz, and many others characterized antislavery activists as a grasping and hypocritical group. They claimed that abolitionists tried to export a system of wage labor for personal profit and disguised their motives by claiming to be concerned with the plight of slaves. Calhoun, for example, in an 1847 speech inveighing against proposed legislation to prohibit slavery in the territories or the admission of new slave states, said, "I will not say whether . . . it has been the work of men, who, looking to political power, have considered the agitation of this question as the most effectual mode of obtaining to spoils of this Government. look to the fact itself. . . . It is a scheme, which aims to monopolize the powers of this Government and to obtain sole possession of its territories" (Calhoun 385).

More recently, historians have reshaped this argument. David Brion Davis, for example, has theorized that antislavery leaders were unconsciously complicit in assuring that workers accepted the wage labor system.[4] Thomas Haskell extended this argument, saying that abolitionists, like the vast majority of their contemporaries, were formalists who believed strongly in the power of individuals to shape their own lives barring legal barriers: "In the eyes of an observer who makes little or no distinction between formal and substantive freedom, legally free workers bear a large measure of responsibility for their own plight, but the suffering of slaves, being wholly involuntary, is the responsibility of everyone who has any power to stop it" (876). As formalists, abolitionists distinguished between the ethical position of slavery, which gave slave owners the legal power to split apart slave families and directly abuse individual slaves, and the ethical position of wage labor, which gave no such direct power to employers. These abolitionists did not acknowledge, or perhaps recognize, that the circumstances of free labor may have deprived wage workers of any option other than entering highly exploitative work contracts.

Other historians have pointed to the many abolitionists who defy this characterization. Edward Magdol has analyzed the composition of the antislavery rank and file and found a preponderance of wage earners, suggesting that they felt the movement had empowering implications for workers. David Roediger describes one group of prominent abolitionists who were not formalists. William Lloyd Garrison, Charles Sumner, Gerrit Smith, Josiah Abbott, Karl Heinzen, and Wendell Phillips collaborated with labor leader Ira Steward on a Radical Republican paper, the *Daily Evening Voice*, advocating both the eight-hour day and African American civil rights after the Civil War. They argued that, even with the formal freedom to negotiate contracts, workers were effectively powerless against heavily capitalized employers who could demand 12-hour days for subsistence wages (Roediger, "Ira Steward").

Ultimately, Lydia Maria Child was a formalist. She did not support protective legislation like the eight-hour law or laws favoring unions. She did recognize, however, the destructive effects of the wage labor system in the absence of the social identity and protections offered by small communities or parishes. She regarded the new wage labor system as inevitable and looked for ways to limit the power of individual self-interest. She saw the means to limit the antisocial tendencies of capitalist individualism in powerful religious and social movements as well as in domestic ideology.[5] Acutely aware of these antisocial tendencies, Child anticipated many later reformers by imagining a "mothering state" as a solution.

A second context in which Child's social theory is to be seen involves the current debate over the development of what Christopher Lasch calls the "social field." The social field developed late in the nineteenth century and comprised an assortment of government agencies as well as more loosely aggregated "experts" who increasingly regulated what traditionally was understood to be a family's affairs. Child's reflections on the emerging Northern economy constitute an early rationale for the growing social field. While Christopher Lasch and Jacques Donzelot, as well as some recent critics of the Progressive Era, see this social field as ultimately disempowering to the working class, Child's early vision of the "mothering state" specifically empowered working-class women and children.[6]

THE INADEQUACY OF THE SEPARATE-SPHERES MODEL

Child's conceptualization of the "mothering state" has its roots in her antislavery fiction, which popularized the figure of the Southern tragic mulatta—a figure that bears a surprising relation to Child's street urchin. These characters emerged simultaneously in Child's writings in the early 1840s, and both point to the inadequacy of the separate-spheres model. At a time when American writers had largely abandoned seduction tales, the stories of tragic mulattas adapted the form of the seduction tale to the antislavery cause. In stories that circulated in gift books and sold at antislavery fairs—stories such as "The Quadroons" (1842) and "Slavery's Pleasant Homes" (1843)—the racially mixed heroine's light skin, European features, and genteel manners make her virtually indistinguishable from the white heroines in women's fiction of the period. Her racial legacy, however, leaves her unable to receive the protection marriage supposedly gives the "true woman" in exchange for obedience to her husband. Despite her modesty and devotion to one man, she cannot ward off the advances of her white owner ("Slavery's Pleasant Homes") or prevent her white "husband" from denying their legally unrecognized marriage and abandoning her ("The Quadroons").

Some critics have read Child's stories about tragic mulattas as an endorsement of the separate-spheres model for African American women, a troubling conclusion given Child's advocacy of more public roles for women in her other writings. Jean Fagan Yellin contends that "these writings, in which she dramatized the sexual oppression of a light-skinned slave, implicitly endorsed for the Tragic Mulatta the restrictive patriarchal ideology of true womanhood—an ideology that Child rejected for herself" (*Women and Sisters* 76). On the contrary, far from endorsing the ideology of separate spheres, Child exposes the extreme and dangerous isolation of both black and white Southern women in the domestic sphere.

The tragedy of Child's mixed-race heroines is in many ways shared by all Southern women in Child's fiction. Without access to a public voice, even the white woman's "patriarchal protections" crumble. For Child, the Southern white woman had little recourse in the face of her husband's infidelities. She, too, was a tragic figure unable to secure the respect and power in the domestic realm promised to the "true woman." In Child's political imagination, Southern women of all races were especially disempowered because of their extreme isolation. She describes one such Southern white woman as having been "nurtured in seclusion, almost as deep as that of the oriental harem" ("Slavery's Pleasant Homes" 238).

Child believed there was a fundamental difference between the position of the family in Northern and Southern society. In the South, the privacy of the family and the weakness of public institutions allowed patriarchs to rule as tyrants. Northern families, in Child's view, were far more subject to the incipient social field represented by public, democratic institutions. In the North, social and structural inequities between genders had been and would continue to be addressed through the press, courts, and schools. Searching for a sign system for representing Northern industrial capitalism, Child never used the seduction tale, despite her interest in several "fallen" women in New York.[7]

Developed simultaneously by Child in the early 1840s, the figures of the tragic mulatta and the street child are closely linked as indicators of trouble in the patriarchal American family. But the Northern street child, a figure that appears frequently in Child's *Letters from New York*, faced a threat far different and more ubiquitous than the one that confronted the tragic mulatta or Southern women more generally. By casting the street urchin outside of a domestic space, in the dangerously free marketplace, Child implied that neither father, husband, owner, nor employer oppressed the child. Family and marketplace did not combine forces in the North to exploit the street child, as they did in the case of the tragic mulatta. If in the South the private realm eclipsed the public and operated according to market logic, in the North it simply evaporated for the working-class child, replaced by an alluring but impersonal marketplace.

Together the figures of the tragic mulatta and the street urchin showed how inadequate both a model of paternalistic agrarianism and a model of liberal self-possession were in the era of emerging industrial capitalism. Contrary to the assertions of agrarians, dependents could not trust the privileges afforded by their "natural" protectors. However, the alternative model of liberal self-possession, in which the fundamental social unit was the individual rather than the family, also threatened social stability. When each individual pursued his or her own self-interest, the result, according to Child, was neither the most efficient nor the most collectively satisfying community.[8]

FROM PAUPERS TO STREET CHILDREN

With her two series of letters during the early 1840s, Child brought to New York her ability to capture social forces in the shorthand of character types. The most industrialized city outside of England, New York was, in historian Christine Stansell's terms, "the historical stage writ large for encounters that reverberated across the rest of the nation" and "a staging ground for the great transformations of the industrial wage system" (xiv, 4). Child peopled this stage, as she peopled the Southern "brothelhouse" in her antislavery fiction, with sensational characters.

In the first installment of the *Letters from New York*, Child describes the city in terms closely related to her antislavery work:

> You ask what is now my opinion of this great Babylon.... The din of crowded life, and the eager chase for gain, still run through its streets, like the perpetual murmur of a hive. Wealth dozes on French couches, thrice piled, and canopied with damask, while Poverty camps on the dirty pavement, or sleeps off its wretchedness in the watch-house. There amid the splendour of Broadway, sits the blind negro beggar, with horny hand and tattered garments, while opposite to him stands the stately mansion of the slave trader, still plying his bloody trade, and laughing to scorn the cobweb laws, through which the strong can break so easily.
>
> (*LNY* 1)

Child attacks the old and new elite (the slave trader is part aristocrat and part merchant) and in the process manages to relate this class conflict to slavery. The frame includes a "negro beggar" outside the slave trader's mansion; however, unlike the slave in conventional abolitionist appeals, this man is not exploited but abandoned. Or rather, he has been both exploited and abandoned; having worked to make the slave trader rich—work his horny hands attest to—he has now been cast loose as a beggar. Child merges the Southern slave and the wage slave in this striking figure.

The *Letters from New York* repeatedly return to the cityscape's dangerous "freedom" in which individuals, far from being fettered, lack the bonds that could lend stability to personal identity during economic downturns. Rather than endorsing capitalist individualism as an alternative to the domestic subjugation under slavery of all but a propertied, white, male elite, Child developed an alternative model based on a democratization of family relations and a new layer of social institutions that would compensate for inadequate family resources.

This first letter quickly moves from the hybrid figure of the "blind negro beggar" to that of the street child. "The noisy discord of the street-cries gives the ear no rest; and the weak voice of weary childhood often makes the heart ache for the poor little wanderer, prolonging his task far into the hours of the night" (1–2). Whether hawking newspapers, matches, or rags, the "little wanderer" invariably demonstrates the tendency of the Northern marketplace to turn the child out of the home and to transform parental affection into indifference.

Child developed the trope of the street urchin to focus her perception of Northern social and economic problems. This figure could elicit a sympathetic response among readers without stimulating class antagonisms in the North.[9] Because the seduction tale became, under Child's influence, a story of class antagonisms in the South (planter vs. slave), it became an effective method of indicting power relations on several axes: race, gender, and class. The street urchin, however, especially as Child developed the figure from her earlier fiction, pointed toward the need for more powerful social institutions—indeed, a maternalist state—rather than the need to curb the power of private patriarchs or, as in the case of the blind negro beggar, of large capitalists. The trope muted the picture of class, racial, or gender antagonisms that might have emerged had Child continued to present contrasting pictures of merchants and beggars like those in her first letter. The street child invariably worked on the fringes of society, not in a large factory where his or her injustices could be directly attributed to an exploitative employer. The street child, as everyone's child, pointed toward the need for parenting structures, a proto-welfare state that would absorb and socialize potentially dangerous, dissatisfied members of society.

LETTERS FROM NEW YORK: TURNING THE FAMILY ROMANCE INSIDE OUT

In the *Letters from New York*, Child rarely pictures impoverished people in domestic settings, and when she does, their homes are anything but ideal. This new pattern marks a break with her previous practice in the *Juvenile Miscellany*, a magazine for children. In Child's earlier stories, the poor lived in homes that resembled those of their more fortunate neighbors, except they had lost one or both parents and struggled to afford basic necessities. Poverty and unjust suffering among the white Northerners in these stories were surmounted by incorporating rich and poor in a single family. In her urban sketches, on the other hand, the poor are no longer unfortunate brothers or sisters but a distinct class having little contact with their more prosperous neighbors. The "all in the family" magical resolution of Child's fiction from the *Juvenile Miscellany* gave way to a vision of the proto-welfare state.[10]

At first, Child struggled to develop a coherent analysis and correspond-ing vocabulary with which to confront industrializing New York. Her personal letters to friends from Boston reflect her sense that New York was both more open and more dangerous than Boston or other American cities.[11] Neither melting pot nor mosaic in her imagination, the city is depicted as a "thoroughfare of nations," suggesting it was less a place than a temporal stage through which one passed—a harbinger of changes to come in other American cities (*LNY* 43). Stansell has called antebellum New York "a way station of Atlantic misery," the main port of entry for immigrants and the industrial and shipping capital of the United States (5). Initially, the city's pace and variety appealed to Child. In June 1841, she wrote to her close friend Ellis Gray Loring that she and John Hopper were "promenading the Battery four nights in the week, until 12 o'clock" (*SL* 145). Child took her views to the public when she wrote admiringly of the city's openness in her second column for *Letters from New York*:

> I like the various small gardens in New-York, with their shaded alcoves of lattice-work, where one can eat an ice-cream, shaded from the sun. You have none such in Boston; and they would probably be objected to, as open to the vulgar and the vicious. I do not walk through the world with such fear of soiling my garments. Let science, literature, music, flowers, all things that tend to cultivate the intellect, or humanize the heart, be open to "Tom, Dick, and Harry;" and thus, in process of time, they will become Mr. Thomas, Richard and Henry.
>
> (*LNY* 6)

The city's frenetic activity, the possibility of great changes in one's for-tunes, and the contact with people of all ethnicities, religions, and classes were very exciting to Child. She even confessed to a preference for New York over her beloved Boston where she believed social mobility to be more limited. Nonetheless, she had her doubts about market capitalism. The very freedom she found appealing for herself was, in her mind, dan-gerous for street children. The extremes of wealth and poverty as well as the social dislocation that isolated the very poor disturbed her throughout her nine years in New York.

She remarks upon the social dislocation she found in her new city:

> More, perhaps, than any other city, except Paris or New Orleans, this is a place of rapid fluctuation, and never-ceasing change.... Where men are little known, they are imperfectly restrained; therefore, great numbers here live with somewhat of that wild license which prevails in times of pestilence. Life is a reckless game, and death is a business transaction. Warehouses of ready-made coffins, stand beside warehouses of ready-made clothing, and the shroud is sold with spangled opera-dresses. Nay, you may chance to see exposed at sheriffs' sales, in public squares, piles of coffins, like nests of boxes, one within another, with a hole bored in the topmost lid to sustain the red flag of the auctioneer, who stands by, describing their conveniences and merits, with all the exaggerating eloquence of his tricky trade. (56–7)

As in Child's antislavery fiction, the auctioneer presides over the marketplace and dehumanizes his victims. In this case, however, it is the customers—whose most deeply felt needs are leveled with their most trivial desires, whose shrouds and opera dresses commingle—who feel the "night-mare sensation of vanishing identity" (57). The marketplace removes the aura from the things people might use to anchor their senses of themselves. Child's "Letters" are preoccupied with Northern economic changes, especially growing disparities of income, social fragmentation, and what she perceived to be the corrupting influence of the "change"— her word for both the market exchange and the specific economic changes in New York City.

By the end of Child's first summer in New York, she had become frightened by the crime reports she read in the penny press. "This New York is a frightful place," she wrote to Loring. "What is the reason the proportion of crime is so much greater than in London? For a good while past, I have walked but little after 10 o'clock at night. I am afraid to . . . [T]he penny papers, every now and then, frighten me out of my wits" (*SL* 147).

Even while Child resisted the paranoid view of the city circulated in the penny papers, she nevertheless repeatedly returned to New York's crime problems as a way of discussing the emerging class structure of this industrial city. Early in the *Letters from New York* series, she says, "The disagreeables of New-York, I deliberately mean to keep out of sight, when I write to you. By contemplating beauty, the character becomes beautiful" (*LNY* 11). Yet Child's "Letters" contain more of New York's crime and poverty than its beautiful sights or cultural events. In fact, crime becomes her subspecialty as she tours a penitentiary, devotes several letters to famous criminal cases, and links crime to the industrializing city's fragmented social structure.[12] She notes that poor neighborhoods are increasingly remote from middle-class neighborhoods, isolating and demoralizing poor youth. Moreover, the new, poor immigrants seldom attend the same churches or schools as middle-class native-born New Yorkers, intensifying their isolation. Visiting the infamous Five Points section of Manhattan, Child says it is worse than "Hogarth's Gin Lane" with its "leer of the licentious, the dull sensualism of the drunkard, the sly glance of the thief" (14). Most disturbing are the many children she sees in the streets: "And *this* is the education society gives her children . . . !" (14). The very geography of New York suggested that social institutions, or the lack thereof, caused both crime and poverty. Five Points was once "a spacious pond of sweet, soft water." But misguided social policy resulted in a blighted, pestilent neighborhood, produced at great social expense. The pond, Child observed,

> might have furnished half the city with the purifying element; but it was filled up at incredible expense. [. . .] This is a good illustration of the policy of society toward crime. Thus does it choke up nature, and then seek to protect itself from the result, by the incalculable expense of bolts, bars, the gallows, watch-houses, police courts, constables, and "Egyptian tombs," as they call one of the principal prisons here. (15)

This is one of several passages in the "Letters" that come surprisingly close to an early form of naturalism in which the neighborhood's physical landscape and the city's commercial culture so demoralizes the inhabitants that their better "natures" are "choked up."[13] Child's focus on children and on the environmental determinants of crime suggests that reformed social structures might prevent crime as well as poverty. What distinguishes the "Letters" from later naturalist works is Child's mode of address. Repeatedly she feels herself being dragged under by the demoralizing influences she describes; she does not assume a gulf between herself, aligned with an enlightened readership, and a brutalized subject lacking self-consciousness. She maintains a delicate and important balance between her contention that "society makes the crime it punishes" and her representation of individuals who, against all probability, transcend their straightened circumstances.[14]

The city initially appears to be a chaotic welter of disparate individuals, a modern Babylon; however, Child comes ultimately to regard it as a system possessing a logic, however inhumane at times, which could be seen, described, and eventually controlled. In one of her longest letters of the series, she gives an account of her 1842 trip to Blackwell's

Island, a penitentiary, and the Long Island Farms, an orphanage located on a neighboring island. Both institutions represented state attempts to quarantine potentially dangerous elements. Child describes the fate of the young men on Blackwell's Island as an industrial catastrophe, the result, in large part, of an inexorable logic and, in some smaller part, of random chance. She wrote,

> The natural, spontaneous influences of society should be such as to supply men with healthy motives, and give full, free play to the affections, and the faculties. It is horrible to see our young men goaded on by the fierce, speculating spirit of the age, from the contagion of which it is almost impossible to escape, and then see them tortured into madness, or driven to crime, by fluctuating changes of the money-market. The young soul is, as it were, entangled in the great merciless machine of a falsely-constructed society; the steam he had no hand in raising, whirls him hither and thither, and it is altogether a lottery chance whether it crushes or propels him. (193–94)

The marketplace is both a microcosm of the city and the machinery for producing the (non) identity of urban youth. It proves so exciting, so compelling, it draws in young people before they have developed the social ties that would restrain their antisocial impulses and develop their inchoate senses of justice. The "great merciless machine" represents the intransigent logic of the market economy, while the steam suggests the random nature of individual outcomes in such a system. Child's industrial metaphor for the mangling of "young souls" shows the extent to which her previous writings on the poor were challenged and revised as a result of her experience in New York City. Whereas the virtuous poor came to the attention of their wealthy and well-meaning neighbors in her previous fiction, such personal intervention was wholly inadequate to the conditions she observed in New York. Instead, she developed a more complex sense of class structure that called into question a simple model of capitalist upward mobility based on the Protestant work ethic.

Before her tour of the Long Island Farm, Child viewed the orphanage as a positive alternative to the crime and drunkenness she saw in infamous New York neighborhoods like Five Points. She commented, "I thought of the squalid little wretches I had seen at Five Points, whose greatest misfortune was that they were not orphans" (56). Child's view of the families of Five Points as a liability to the development of their children fell into the state-guardianship model of child rearing fostered by social reformers Robert Dale Owen and Frances Wright. These reformers had a dim view of immigrant and working-class cultures and proposed eliminating nuclear families to protect children from the negative influences of their parents.[15]

But Child revised her view of state institutions as she investigated the prisons and orphanages of New York in greater depth. The very location of Blackwell's Island and the Long Island Farm, in the East River off Manhattan, suggested their limitations. They quarantined those already suffering from social isolation. Regarding the children at Long Island Farm, Child noted, "The drawbacks are such as inevitably belong to their situation, as children of the public. The oppressive feeling is, that there are no mothers there. Every thing [*sic*] moves by machinery, as it always must with masses of children, never subdivided into families" (197). Viewing the economy as a machine, she imagined the state in a similar fashion sundering the social bonds that might provide the basis for self-esteem and social control. She discovered that the boys were daily drilled in military exercises, that everyone dropped to their knees for prayers when a whistle blew, and that the children were forbidden to speak as they dressed in the morning. She commented, "Alas, poor childhood, thus doth 'church and state' provide for thee! The state arms thee with wooden guns, to play the future murderer, and the church teaches thee to pray in platoons" (197).

In her view of orphan asylums, Child departs from the prevailing wisdom and, especially, as David J. Rothman notes, from positions taken by other child-rearing advisors of the period. "The asylum's primary task," Rothman asserts, "was to teach an absolute respect for authority through the establishment and enforcement of a rigorous and orderly routine." Influential advice writers such as John and Jacob Abbott, William Alcott, and Catharine Beecher wrote popular child-rearing manuals shot through with endorsements of strict parental discipline and an absolute deference to authority from children.[16] Child's understanding that crime stemmed less from permissive parenting than from social isolation led her to different solutions to urban crime and poverty, solutions reminiscent of those measures promoted by Progressive Era reformers.

Child believed that orphaned children were conditioned by the same forces that created juvenile delinquents. Unlike other reformers, she pointed beyond inadequate parenting to environmental factors. Physically unhealthy living conditions and alienation from major social institutions fed a general demoralization among the population of Five Points. One newspaper boy she met, a four-year-old with a voice "prematurely cracked into shrillness," she followed in her imagination

> to the miserable cellar where he probably slept on dirty straw; I saw him flogged, after his day of cheerless toil, because he had failed to bring home pence enough for his parents' grog; I saw wicked ones come muttering and beckoning between his young soul and heaven; they tempted him to steal, to avoid the dreaded beating. I saw him, years after, bewildered and frightened, in the police-office, surrounded by hard faces [...]. At that

moment, one tone like a mother's voice might have wholly changed his earthly destiny.

(LNY 83)

This "gallows game" between the hard law, the multitudes laughing at the police reports, and the youthful offender never given reason to respect the law was a circuitous game, according to Child. "When, oh when," she says repeatedly in the "Letters," "will men learn that society makes and

Figure 2.1   "More big as he could carry." Lewis Hines photographed working children, including this newsboy in 1910. Courtesy of the Library of Congress.

cherishes the very crimes it so fiercely punishes, and *in* punishing reproduces?" (84). Again and again, Child describes desperately poor children hawking newspapers or matches, alone or accompanied by demoralized, detached mothers (see figure 2.1). Her confidence in her ability to read the past and future of a person based on a momentary meeting is a part of her growing understanding of poverty as a systemic, rather than personal, failure. The ragged newspaper boy, the matchbox girl, the drunken woman picked up by the constables all were determined by their social position. Unlike the poor depicted in Child's early fiction, these poor had little power to resist the juggernaut of economic change.[17]

"HOME IS THE COMMUNITY"

What Child envisioned instead of prison or orphanage was a society in which "no human being [grew] up without deep and friendly interest from the society round him" (193). The Society of Friends, Child noted, operated a community in which the old, the ill, and the orphaned were taken care of by an intimate society in which none felt like a burden because all would have likewise helped their neighbors.[18] As Child imagined this system applied in the city, however, it lost some of its egalitarian qualities. She envisioned a disciplinary apparatus with "a mother's voice." Child's discourse and her specific reform agenda anticipated what historians have called "maternalist" social policies. Seth Koven and Sonya Michel coined this term to describe "the political discourses and strategies" used by Progressive Era women who "transformed motherhood from women's primary *private* responsibility into *public* policy" (2). Nearly 50 years before Jane Addams founded Hull House and 60 before Florence Kelley founded the National Consumer's League, devoted to raising the minimum wage and limiting the number of hours women and children could work, Child adapted domestic discourse to a progressive political agenda (see figure 2.2). During the 1840s, domestic discourse became, overall, increasingly conservative; women's magazines and domestic fiction ceased to endorse the benevolent organizations from which antislavery and feminism had initially sprung. Child, however, was developing a new discourse that would sanction women's first roles within the state.

Child is in many ways representative of radical abolitionists who lauded "free society" but were nevertheless critical of the wage relationship. Whereas some antislavery activists believed their work complete with the emancipation of slaves, she believed there was much more to be done. Along with antislavery activists like Frederick Douglass and Wendell Phillips, Child developed a program for social reform following the Civil War that extended beyond formal citizenship rights for African

Figure 2.2   Jane Addams reading to immigrant children. Courtesy of the Wisconsin Historical Society (WHi-6126).

Americans. Her program exceeded the minimalist reforms that might have fallen within the interests of the emerging bourgeoisie. Presidential Reconstruction, for example, left former slaves to fend for themselves without economic resources or power within major social institutions. In contrast, Child's education initiatives, her support for the Freedmen's Bureau, and her support for land redistribution all aimed at building the civil society and African American cohesion that her experience of New York City during the 1840s told her would be essential to the freedmen's empowerment.[19]

Child's specific post-Civil War reform agenda shows the influence of her study of New York's social structure. She compiled a primer for teaching freed African Americans to read that included 18 pieces by 11 African American authors. Published in 1865, *The Freedmen's Book* also featured the biographies of accomplished African Americans. Child hoped the collection would provide a "true record of what colored men have accomplished, under great disadvantages" (preface). In other words, she believed that a sense of collective pride, of belonging to a larger community, was crucial to individual advancement. Moreover, she actively advocated federal financial support of the Freedmen's Bureau. Among the responsibilities of the bureau was the negotiation of fair labor contracts, the establishment of African American schools and churches, and the reunification of African American families separated by the slave market and war. The last two measures, in particular, were aimed at stimulating an effective, permanent civil society within which African Americans could form and effectively advance community interests.

As part of the modernizing vanguard, Child advanced a new vision of the relationship between public and familial realms through her fictional treatment of Northern and Southern society. In her 1843 image of the "blind negro beggar," she exhibited her twin concerns with slavery—the possession of one person by another—and with wage labor—the dispossession and social abandonment of individuals in the marketplace. Not only did material bonds between slaves and slaveholders have to be severed, but the civil society that would empower and embrace freed slaves would have to be strengthened. Women and men tried to build state institutions that would cushion the marketplace by extending the reach of mothering.

Child was an integral part of the ideological transformation that produced the modern family. As a writer of children's fiction and several advice books aimed at mothers and housewives (*The Frugal Housewife* [1829], *The Mother's Book* [1831], *The Girl's Own Book* [1833], *The Family Nurse* [1837]), she trained women to produce self-disciplined children and to save for their children's education, both crucial prerequisites to modern, middle-class family life. As a social critic concerned with street children, she advocated reforms in the criminal justice system, including a less punitive but more extensive program for intervening with juvenile delinquents.

Jacques Donzelot and Christopher Lasch view this movement toward a more direct governmental intervention in family dynamics as a disempowering one, particularly for working-class people.[20] Christopher Lasch is especially critical of the forces disciplining the modern American family. He writes, "The socialization of production—under the control of private industry—proletarianized the labor force in the same way that the socialization of reproduction proletarianized parenthood, by making people unable to provide for their own needs without the supervision of trained experts" (19).

The social field Lasch and Donzelot view as an oppressive force, however, in many instances augmented the power and material well-being of the working class as they lost much control over the workplace. Child's "maternalist" discourse and political ideology prepared Americans to accept an enlarged social field, encompassing the "trained experts" Lasch cites as well as social reforms primarily benefiting the working class, such as child labor laws, minimum wages, shorter hours, safer work conditions, unemployment insurance, mothers' pensions, and public education (Sklar

68–71). Moreover, women of all classes found avenues for empowerment in these new social programs.

Child used the figure of the tragic mulatta, and the seduction tale more generally, to characterize slavery as a violation of modern family norms. Not only did slavery necessitate the incursion of the market-place into familial relations, but it also precluded the development of the social field, the buffering apparatus meant to supplement and condition familial relations. Child's antislavery arguments and iconography aimed at both curbing the unfettered power of the laissez-faire market-place and developing a social field that would ameliorate the isolation and poverty stemming from a more extensive, more powerful marketplace. Many Northerners who resisted appeals based on the suffering within the Southern family responded to the closely related problem of the South's truncated civil society and social field. Attempts by proslavery men to interfere with the mail, infringe rights of public assembly, curtail freedom of the press, and even assault American senators (Charles Sumner's beating in the Senate aroused many) drew fence-sitters to the abolitionists' ranks. Frederick Law Olmsted struck a devastating blow with his profile of the South, *The Cotton Kingdom*. Olmsted indicted the South for failing to produce the civil society necessary to support democracy; the South had proportionately far fewer public schools, libraries, printing presses, benevolent societies, churches, and lecture and concert halls.[21]

Abolitionists like Child encouraged the development of a "maternal-ist state" that made economic liberalism more palatable. She would laud the wage relationship in public comparisons between North and South. In a widely reprinted exchange of letters between Child and Margaretta Mason, wife of Virginia senator James Mason, Mrs. Mason compared the selfishness of Northern women with the generosity of Southern women. She specifically cited the example of Southern women who cared for female slaves in childbirth and one who stayed up all night sewing a Christmas gown for "a motherless child." Child's searing reply endorsed wage labor in the following terms:

> We pay our domestics generous wages, with which they can purchase as many Christmas gowns as they please; a process far better for their char-acters, as well as our own, than to receive their clothing as a charity, after being deprived of just payment for their labor. I have never known an instance where the "pangs of maternity" did not meet with requisite assistance; and here at the North, after we have helped the mothers, *we do not sell the babies.*
>
> ("Reply of Mrs. Child" 251)

Here then was the crux of the issue for Child. If the laws were not prejudiced against a class of people, they could sell their labor for "just payment." Child believed in social and economic mobility, provided laws and customs did not deprive individuals of opportunity. She believed, however, in delivering "requisite assistance" that was not the patronizing charity of the exploiters toward the defrauded but the reciprocal obligation of citizens toward one another. By choosing the street child to represent the working class, rather than a popular figure such as the starving seamstress, Child suggested that children who felt the "deep and friendly interest" of their society would themselves go on to offer assistance when they were grown.

Jacques Donzelot and Christopher Lasch describe the development of this social field, and especially the social welfare state, in negative terms. Donzelot's term "policing state" emphasizes the surveillance and regulating functions of social welfare programs, downplaying the very real power labor and working-class organizations secured during the development of the "welfare state." Neither Donzelot nor Lasch considers the linkages between social welfare and labor legislation as the two emerged together in America.

Pace Donzelot and Lasch, in the American context, social welfare programs emerged to empower women as mothers and to empower the working class.[22] In her analysis of women's role in the formation of social welfare programs in the United States, Great Britain, France, and Germany, Kathryn Kish Sklar explains the late emergence of such programs in the United States. White male Americans gained equal political rights before the development of a working class. Consequently, male political culture did not support a working-class political party during the period when social welfare programs were developed in comparable Western countries. However, in France, Germany, and Great Britain, labor and socialist parties emerged to fight for universal male suffrage and other political rights. These same parties, along with powerful labor unions, developed social welfare programs and advocated them as working-class rights. Workers' compensation, unemployment insurance, regulations for workplace safety, child-labor laws, widows' and mothers' pensions, and state-funded health care were measures passed by European legislatures responding to pressure from working-class males. In the United States, these social welfare programs were developed and eventually passed through a partnership between grassroots organizations led by middle-class women and individual male political leaders.

Antebellum female reform, of which Child was such an important leader, provided the organization and the discourse that pushed through the first parts of social welfare legislation in the United States. The first large-scale national program provided widows' and mothers' pensions to the wives of working-class men killed in dangerous industrial work. As Sklar notes,

> One striking peculiarity of the process by which the welfare state emerged in the United States before 1930 was the degree to which widespread mobilization of middle-class women on behalf of legislation to improve the working conditions of wage-earning women became an entering wedge for the extension of state responsibility to wage-earning men and to other aspects of women's lives (such as maternal health). (50)

In a country in which a tradition of limited government, weak class identification, and hostility to labor actions impeded the development of social welfare programs, female political culture used maternalist discourse to develop programs primarily benefiting and empowering the working class. Sklar concludes that during the Progressive Era "gender—women's organizations and female-specific legislation—achieved much that in other industrializing nations was done through, and in the name of, class" (75). If Child did not yet recognize the necessity of an organized working-class response to the "socialization of production," she did sense the necessity of an organized community response to the poverty and atomization characteristic of industrialization. Far from disempowering workers, the "socialization of reproduction" filled a vacuum left by laissez-faire economic policies. The movement to provide widows' and mothers' pensions was the beginning of efforts to provide safety regulations in the workplace. The movement to provide state resources for the medical care of mothers and children led to programs providing medical care to disabled and retired workers.

From her position as an antislavery activist, Child influenced the maternalist arguments and figures that a later generation of women reformers would use to justify their pioneering inroads into government on behalf of working-class women, children, and, eventually, men. As an influential activist and propagandist, she is central to the development of women's political culture. Her attempts to establish a regular and personalized correspondence with her readers as well as her conviction that urban poverty should be approached by strengthening community ties between classes were strategies taken up by women reformers 50 years later. Jane Addams, the founder of Hull House in Chicago, the most famous American settlement house, described the mission of the settlement movement in language very similar to Child's: residents "are bound to regard the entire life of their city as organic, to make an effort to unify it, and to make a protest against its overdifferentiation" (100). Suffragist

and Progressive Era reformer Rheta Childe Dorr questioned the boundaries between public and private: "Woman's place is in the Home, but
Home is not contained within the four walls of an individual home.
Home is the community" (qtd. in Diner 202). Imagining herself as a
public mother, Child advocated a more public role for women in guiding
social policy.

Child's tales of the tragic mulatta and those of the street urchin operated together to endorse both the evolving system of wage labor and the
growing social field. If the tragic mulatta indicted the South for its underdeveloped social field and civil society, the street urchin encouraged social
reforms as an extension of "mothering." Both called the ideology of separate spheres into question. Child's vision of a "mothering state" constitutes
a crucial step toward the modern family and the modern social welfare
state. Anticipating later Progressive Era maternalist discourse, Child promoted controversial social reforms in the antebellum era through familiar
icons and narratives, making them coherent and appealing to a wide range
of American readers.

PART 2

ADAPTATIONS OF THE ANTISLAVERY FAMILY PROTECTION CAMPAIGN

CHAPTER 3

MARKETPLACE POLITICS IN *THE SCARLET LETTER*

> She fled for refuge, as it were, to the public exposure

Nathaniel Hawthorne was not an abolitionist. In fact, he was openly hostile to abolitionism and an active Democrat when the Republican Party's radical wing was abolitionist. It is, therefore, remarkable that Hawthorne's most famous novel, *The Scarlet Letter*, should reveal antislavery iconography and a sympathy for the slave and the radical, both embodied by Hester Prynn. Hawthorne's immersion in antislavery discourse as a member of New England's intellectual elite in the 1840s and 1850s influenced his artistry and his emotional predisposition to the plight of the slave even while his party commitments, material interests, and intellectual positions resisted antislavery doctrine. Hawthorne's identification with Hester, an identification at times seemingly involuntary, provides an index for his involuntary sympathy for radicalism, especially for the antislavery family protection campaign. *The Scarlet Letter* demonstrates the power of antislavery sentimentality and, in particular, the way it spoke to the anxiety-ridden lower-middle class in this period of poletarianization.

The identification Hawthorne felt with Hester can first be seen in "The Custom House," Hawthorne's introduction to *The Scarlet Letter*. He complains of his humiliation when dismissed as surveyor of the Salem Custom House and yet describes himself as a resigned "Salemite" whose return to Salem was like a "destiny" so "instinctual" was his attachment to the place. *The Scarlet Letter*'s Hester, too, is held up to public ridicule and yet cannot pull herself away from Boston: "... [I]t may seem marvelous that this woman should still call that place her home where, and where only, she must needs be the type of shame" (Hawthorne, *The Scarlet Letter* 86). Long preoccupied with the significance of his famous family history and name, Hawthorne created in Hester a similar struggle with her own legacy and the way in which it has left her marked.

In the second instance of identification Hawthorne suggests that both he and Hester are victims of a French Revolution-style vicious mob. He positions Hester multiple times on the scaffold and compares his dismissal as surveyor of the Salem Custom House to a "beheading." As Larry Reynolds has rightly recognized, Hawthorne borrowed from the semiotics of the French Revolution to represent his politically motivated firing.[1] Hawthorne positions himself as a mainstream American battling the Whig bureaucracy, figured as blood-thirsty Jacobins. Moreover, the fierce eagle above the Custom House door represents a debilitating socialism; this eagle mother alternately encourages dependence and then "fling[s] off her nestlings, with a scratch of her claw, a dab of her beak, or a rankling wound from her barbed arrows" ("The Custom House" 4). Hester is similarly portrayed on the scaffold before an angry mob calling for gruesome physical punishment at the opening of *The Scarlet Letter*. Reynolds concludes, ". . . [T]hrough the first twelve chapters, half of the book, Hester is dealt with sympathetically as she represents, like Charles I, Louis XVI, and Surveyor Hawthorne, a fallen aristocratic order struggling in defense of her rights against an antagonistic populace" (91). Reynolds argues that the second half of the book characterizes Hester as radical and temptress, an embodiment of Liberty and Eve, as she refuses the Puritan theocracy's laws and tempts Arthur Dimmesdale to do the same.

What is most remarkable here is how the plot of *The Scarlet Letter* challenges the French Revolution's iconography with which Hawthorne began. If Hester becomes Liberty or Eve, as Reynolds contends, then readers would expect her to be behind the beheading machine, not the victim on the scaffold. Repeatedly, Hester appears on the scaffold with her daughter, threatened with separation and silently bearing witness against Puritan law. Even as the narrator becomes more critical of Hester's radical thinking, readers gain more respect for her actions, as she defends the well-being of her daughter and courageously goes forth into a hostile public to care for the sick and to support her child. Morton Cronin credits Hester's "overwhelming appeal" for the narrator's failure to convert with his moralizing (90). He explains,

> The fact is that Hester Prynne is a greater Romantic heroine than Hawthorne deserved. Somehow or other she acquired a life of her own and fought her creator to a standstill. Hawthorne perhaps did not realize

that Romanticism gains its converts not by argument but by example and experience. One experiences Hester as one does not experience Hawthorne's moralizing. (91)

Hester's presence on the scaffold reminds readers of the many antislavery depictions of mothers and children offered for sale in slave markets. Carefully measured and assessed by the Puritans in the marketplace, Hester's situation compels the narrator even as the narrator expresses criticism of her resistance to Puritan law. She is a compelling representation of the antinomian, evidence of the success of the antislavery counter-hegemonic campaign.

Why would Nathaniel Hawthorne, famous for his resistance to feminists and abolitionists, give Hester the antinomian such sympathetic treatment? Hawthorne's attitudes toward slavery and antislavery reformers vacillated. While he was very critical of reformers, whom he characterized as meddlesome and emotionally unbalanced, he admitted to feeling disturbed by the oppression of African Americans in the North. After seeing free African Americans abused and insulted at a public gathering in 1838, Hawthorne revealed in his notebook, "On the whole, I find myself rather more of an abolitionist in feeling than in principle" (*American Notebooks* 48). His visceral response to the scene reveals Hawthorne's vulnerability to the icons of antislavery, which operated on a more emotional, less intellectual level. Even while he publicly resisted the specific arguments the movement advanced, he privately could be swayed by provocative scenes.

The tenuous logic by which Northern anti-abolitionists conceived of themselves as defenders of democracy against fanatical abolitionists gave rise to silence on some issues, hysterical outbursts on others, and a series of moral accommodations and displaced narratives.[2] Hawthorne's relative silence on the issue of slavery and vacillating response to African Americans reveals an ambivalence that made direct, public statements on slavery very difficult.[3] In 1835, as part of a nostalgic article on the history of Salem, he attempted humor as he commented upon the separation of slave families:

> But the slaves we suspect were the merriest part of the population, since it was their gift to be merry in the worst of circumstances; and they endured, comparatively, few hardships, under the domestic sway of our fathers.... When the slaves of a family were inconveniently prolific,—it being not quite orthodox to drown the superfluous offspring, like a litter of kittens,—notice was promulgated of "a negro child to be given away."
> ("Old News" 167)[4]

Hawthorne doubles back on statements. The slaves had a gift for being merry in the "worst of circumstances"—but he quickly adds that they experienced few hardships. The actor is conspicuously absent from the phrase "notice was promulgated" of slave children for sale, even while "our fathers" imposed few hardships. Such indirection and outright contradiction indicate Hawthorne's difficulty in reconciling his own attachment to "our fathers" with their cruelty and the supposed indifference slaves might feel for members of their families.

Hawthorne's ambivalence toward his own identity, as an active political party member, and toward slavery, as a public issue, are linked according to critic Jennifer Fleischner. Hawthorne was not only anti-abolitionist but antipolitical. He believed political life to be degrading, and yet, he was deeply involved in the Democratic Party, carrying out a kickback scheme that required his employees to contribute to the Democratic Party and supporting to the Democratic Party paper (Herbert 162). Nowhere is this twinned ambivalence toward public life and slavery more apparent than in Hawthorne's campaign biography of his college classmate Franklin Pierce. In his introduction to Pierce's 1852 biography, Hawthorne claimed to be uniquely qualified to write on controversial issues because of his political noninvolvement. In one letter, Hawthorne even referred to the artist's vocation as a kind of "priesthood" that required a chaste aloofness from politics (Herbert 162). Fleischner argues that Hawthorne's separation of art and politics mirrored the Democratic Party's separation of antislavery sentiment and federal politics. In the Pierce biography, which supported the Compromise of 1850, antislavery sentiment was a private conviction, not a matter for federal legislation. The Compromise required the privatization of slavery. So long as plebiscites determined the status of newly organized states, the federal government could, conceivably, stay out of the issue of slavery and thereby hold the union together. In other words, privatizing slavery would keep the federal government seemingly innocent of its perpetuation. Of course, the Fugitive Slave Law, implying as it did the cooperation of the free states and the federal government in enforcing slave ownership, suggested that behind such privatization was the very real power of the federal government. The same kind of displacement that permitted Hawthorne to pose as the "priestly" artist and still disseminate his political views permitted the federal government to pose as an innocent bystander to slavery.

Unresolved tensions within Hawthorne's political vision left him acutely vulnerable to the family protection campaign launched by abolitionists. The sensational nature of the family protection campaign specifically targeted those inured to antislavery's well-developed and often repeated arguments. Hawthorne's novel seems designed to refute much of the family protection campaign, and yet, he is unable fully to escape the visceral sympathy his narrator and readers feel for Hester, the beleaguered mother and political mute. *The Scarlet Letter* reveals a deeply contradictory political vision, though many critics find in the novel a consistently conservative politics.

Jean Fagan Yellin and Sacvan Bercovitch, in particular, argue that the novel closes off radical impulses and ultimately champions the conservative, disciplinary mechanisms of the Salem theocracy. Both critics accurately link Hawthorne's Democratic politics to the novel's representation of Hester as an "unruly individual," out of sympathy with the majority of her fellow townspeople. Changes in custom came—for antebellum Democrats and for Hawthorne—not through reforms led by misguided "antinomians" but in "heaven's time." Both Yellin and Bercovitch focus on the first scene in the marketplace, when Hester's community and especially its women cast her out, and the conclusion, when the narrator says that Hester ultimately counsels women to patiently bear their discontent. Both critics argue that Hester, in choosing to return to Salem and wear the scarlet letter, embraces her community's interpretation of her "sin." She believes she has not only broken the Puritan law against adultery but that she has sinned; according to Yellin and Bercovitch, her community has succeeded in persuading Hester not only to consent to their laws but to believe in the fundamental truth of those laws. Thus, Hawthorne succeeds in showing the error of "antinomian" resistance, which arrogantly presumes that individuals can unilaterally determine moral law. By novel's end, according to Yellin and Bercovitch, Hester renounces her claim that, despite the community and biblical injunctions against adultery, her affair with Dimmesdale had "a consecration of its own" (215).

Hawthorne's portrait of Hester, however, ultimately undercuts this reading. Hester, like the nonresistant Garrisonians, respects the rule of law, even if she disputes the specific laws that condemn her affair with Dimmesdale. Even as she suffers from her stigma, she wears the scarlet letter the ministers assign as her punishment. Nonresistants accepted their punishment as martyrs to a righteous cause; in the most famous antebellum exercise of nonresistant martyrdom, Henry David Thoreau refused to pay taxes to support the Mexican War, accepting a night in jail to demonstrate his opposition to a specific law while showing his support for the operation of Law. Garrisonians repeatedly championed the motto "One and God make a majority" to mark their conviction that there was a higher law one should obey even if such obedience resulted in punishment and ostracism.

Yellin examines this portrait of Hester in her groundbreaking *Women and Sisters* and finds in *The Scarlet Letter*'s first scaffold scene a rearticulation of a well-known, feminist, antislavery icon. The slave woman and her child at public auction, threatened with separation, appealed to the "sisterhood" of American women to rise against slavery and in defense of the slave family's integrity. The familiar tableau of a slave woman in the marketplace also suggested her vulnerability to sexual exploitation. Like the slave woman, the feminist abolitionists argued, the free woman could be reduced to a commodity in the marriage market. Antislavery feminists found in the icon a powerful analog to their own sense of enslavement at the hands of patriarchal marriage customs, child custody laws, and property laws. Hawthorne, Yellin claims, used this antislavery icon to condemn both the agenda and the methods of the feminist abolitionists.

> Although his book ends with a kind of restoration of Hester as a Woman and a Sister, she does not achieve this identity by asserting the antislavery feminists' ideology or by struggling for her rights in the public sphere. Instead, learning that she should accept her lot, confident that someday, somehow, things will change for the better, Hester conforms at last to patriarchal definitions of womanhood.
>
> (Yellin 126)

Rather than condemning "the institutional violation of an individual" implicit in Hester's ostracism, as well as slavery and the legal status of women in the nineteenth century, the novel, according to Yellin, ultimately endorses Hester's dehumanizing punishment (137). It is this very dehumanization that eventually leads to her penitence and social regeneration.

In fact, the novel may be read as an endorsement of both the agenda and the methods of the feminist abolitionists. Hester spends her time on the scaffold in the opening scene contemplating the "entire track along which she had been treading" (63) toward that moment, most prominently her awareness that her impoverished family has sold her into marriage with Roger Chillingworth, an older man for whom she feels respect but also physical repugnance. By novel's end Hester has not returned to Chillingworth and has successfully asserted her right and ability to support her daughter. Moreover, Hester does indeed publicly resist her dehumanization on the scaffold in the very way that feminist abolitionists resisted slavery—by using the marketplace, family spectacle, and everyday practices to resist her exclusion from public speaking platforms and to insist upon her right to reject her marriage and keep her daughter.

Hawthorne, as a downwardly mobile lower-middle-class man in 1850, was susceptible to the antislavery family protection campaign because of his own sense of having to barter more than his labor or time in the marketplace.

He felt he had lost some more essential quality by agreeing to affix his initials to standardized commodities traveling through the Custom House. He imagined his characters contemptuously taunting him: "The little power you might once have possessed over the tribe of unrealities is gone. You have bartered it for a pittance of the public gold. Go, then, and earn your wages!" ("The Custom House" 38). Hawthorne feared that he had sold not only his time but some quality essential to his creative abilities:

> It was not merely during the three hours and a half which Uncle Sam claimed as his share of my daily life that this wretched numbness held possession of me. . . . An entire class of susceptibilities, and a gift connected with them—of no great richness or value, but the best I had—was gone from me. (39–40)

Hawthorne's alienated labor, his routine, clerical work, forced him into a Bartleby-like passivity. Yet without the Custom House position, Hawthorne would have been unable to support his family.[5] He identified with Hester as she resists the Puritans' punishment, lavishing her talents on the embroidered "A" on her breast to complicate the simple meaning they meant it to convey. Because of his own tenuous position in the middle class, Hawthorne responded sympathetically to the antislavery critique of human commodification.

Just as Hawthorne could not use antislavery icons in his work without conveying their ideology, increasingly Democrats found it difficult to respond to antislavery discourse and radical Republicans. Material conditions limited what Sacvan Bercovitch has called "free enterprise democracy of symbol making" (Bercovitch 92). By 1850, the symbol of the woman and child on the auction block could not be made to carry a proslavery or even an accommodationist message that would persuade the majority of Americans. While Bercovitch recognizes that compromise and consensus fall through shortly after the Compromise of 1850, he mistakenly attributes this to a failure of rhetoric and "symbol making":

> After 1852, with Webster's death and the struggle for the Free states, the central cultural symbols shifted steadily to embrace the armies of the North, wielding God's terrible swift sword to cut the gordian knot of consent/concession.
>
> Not the ends but the means had changed. Compromise, "to bind by mutual agreement," had failed to provide either the mechanism for binding

or the metaphors for agreement, and with due alacrity the leaders of the
dominant culture had moved to preserve the Union against the hazards of
ambiguity. (102)

Compromise did not fail because Hawthorne or the Democrats could
not find the appropriate metaphor to reconcile slave interests to those
of the working and middle classes in the North. Compromise failed
because the Democratic Party's libertarian paradigm left slaveholder interests in direct conflict with those of workers and the middle class in the
newly organizing western territories.[6] Hawthorne's refusal of the historical romance formula, which would have reincorporated Hester or Pearl
in Puritan society, indicates his own fears that rifts in American society
could not be deferred indefinitely. He does not provide a "metaphor"
through which a unified nation could be imagined. Unlike Lydia Maria
Child, who would write *A Romance of the Republic*, a post–Civil War
historical romance showing the nation healed through an interracial
marriage, Hawthorne and the Democratic Party could not provide a persuasive antebellum vision of the "national family" that also represented the
enslaved. Paternalistic visions of family life in slavery were belied by the
more prevalent spectacle of the slave market. Abolitionists successfully disseminated images of the slave family on the scaffold, images that took root
because of a heightened sense of the family's fragility and importance.[7]
Not until after the Civil War would images of fratricidal conflict replace
this powerful icon of mother and child in the slavemart in the national
imagination.

NATHANIEL HAWTHORNE'S REARTICULATION OF ANTISLAVERY ICONOGRAPHY

Finding the appropriate metaphor or trope *within* the "limits and pressures" of economic forces could be enormously persuasive.[8] Antislavery
activists were masters of rearticulation, the process of taking popular
icons, stories, or revered texts and turning them to antislavery purposes.[9]
The Bible, the Declaration of Independence, Winthrop's "Model of
Christian Charity"—all could be used as tools in the campaign against
slavery. Even Southern, proslavery newspapers contained antislavery tools,
as Theodore Dwight Weld and the Grimke sisters discovered when they
compiled the popular *American Slavery As It Is*, an encyclopedic collection of clippings from Southern newspapers grouped by categories like
"Brandings," "Cruelties," and "Wanton Cruelties." The abolitionists carried this tactic one step further when they republished pictures from
Southern papers depicting slavery.

In the July 1836 edition of *The Anti-Slavery Record*, a slave of uncertain sex stands on the auction block (see cover). Clipped from a Southern newspaper advertising slaves for sale, the drawing was published shortly after the monthly American Anti-slavery Society publication was excoriated in Congress for its "incendiary" pictures of slavery's abuses. Proslavery congressmen exhibited an assortment of antislavery publications, claiming the pictures within were "calculated, in an eminent degree, to rouse and inflame the passions of the slaves against their masters" (qtd. in Miller 97). Responding to accusations that the pictures were unrepresentative of Southern slave society, contributors to the *Record* reprinted this picture with the following inscription: "Now, how does it come to pass, that this said picture when printed in a southern newspaper is perfectly harmless, but when printed in *The Anti-Slavery Record* is perfectly incendiary? We have nothing further to say about it till this question is answered" ("Who Bids? Incendiary Pictures").

This simple, rough sketch of a featureless slave as commodity and spectacle, the editors suggest, is neither a misrepresentation nor a sensational drawing. The sign's meaning is contingent upon how readers are trained to see these pictures. The editors refuse to interpret the sign or comment upon it, leaving it to the viewer to question how various readers are trained to see black people and slave relations. While the slave trader or owner may read this sign and the black figure in it instrumentally, noting the time and place of the slave auction, the presumably more ethical reader of *The Anti-Slavery Record* would see in the hunched, black figure a human degraded by his or her commodification.

The Anti-Slavery Record worked to de-naturalize such signs by placing them in the context of stories of seduction, betrayal, and tyranny. The first step in such a campaign was to insist upon the humanity of slaves. Because the slave in "Who bids?" is pictured in the marketplace, the sketch would have seemed familiar to the *Record*'s readers, but the slave's featureless face and sexless form stand in stark contrast to the other sketches included in the *Record*. Other pictures dramatize the anguish of mothers separated from children and the dire results of slavery's stress upon family relations (see figure 3.1).

Defenders of slavery tended to suppress speech rather than rearticulate antislavery discourse or icons. Though some used the Bible, the Constitution, and the safety of white families in the South as defenses of slavery, far more memorable were techniques like the gag rule tabling antislavery petitions in Congress, the persecution of antislavery speakers, the burning of presses, and the interdiction of antislavery mailings. Anti-abolitionists refused to engage antislavery signs and arguments, resorting to ad hominem attacks and caricatures of blacks and reformers.[10]

52

THE

ANTI-SLAVERY RECORD.

VOL. I.   MAY, 1835.   NO. 5.

CRUELTIES OF SLAVERY.

When we narrate the cruelties of individual masters upon their slaves, it is not for the purpose of exciting public indignation against those masters, nor of drawing the inference, that all masters are equally cruel; but to show that cruelty is the fruit of the system. Every tree must be known by its fruits. Cruelty may occur under good and impartial laws, but then it is in spite of the laws, not in consequence of them. On the other hand, where the laws themselves violate rights, make one class the property of another, and withhold redress of wrongs, cruelty, in ten thousand forms, is the necessary result. If the amount of cruelty perpetrated upon the slaves of this republic could be known to the world,

Vol. I.   5

Figure 3.1   "Cruelties of Slavery" was the cover image for the May 1835 edition of *The Anti-Slavery Record*. Courtesy of Special Collections, University of Virginia Library

Hawthorne's rearticulation of the scaffold scene in *The Scarlet Letter* is one of the few examples of an anti-abolitionist using a specifically antislavery sign.[11]

Few have recognized Hester's resemblance to the slave woman with her child on the block, in part because Hawthorne's novel is set in seventeenth-century Salem and in part because Hawthorne seldom dealt explicitly with the issue of slavery in his writing. Leland S. Person rectifies this omission in noting that Hester's infanticidal thoughts, her disempowered position relative to the father of her child, and her daughter's fate, following the "condition of her mother," all make Hester similar to slave mothers.[12] In Hawthorne's "family romance," slavery—as a public and private concern, an economic institution and a family matter—places "limits" and "pressures" on Hawthorne's understanding of the emerging domestic ideology. Because antislavery discourse was so prevalent in New England in the late 1840s, the language and iconography of the debate structured how Hawthorne felt and understood other issues.[13] Hawthorne may not have *consciously* articulated Hester's battle for custody of Pearl and her struggle against social annihilation in the iconography of antislavery. The icon of the woman and child on the marketplace scaffold was so powerful, however, that even Hawthorne, resistant as he was to the tactics and arguments of feminist abolitionists, viewed women's political culture through the language of antislavery.

Antislavery iconography appears in Hawthorne's work because of his investment in an emerging middle-class ideology, which valued family privacy and challenged more traditional, contractual views of marriage.[14] The slave family was an increasingly important trope for displaced concern about family structure in the new economic order of the antebellum North. The fractured family of Hawthorne's novel takes much of its emotional power from its resemblance to the dramas and icons of separated slave families in antislavery materials. Hawthorne's representation of Hester and her successful resistance to the Puritan theocracy shows the extent to which antislavery iconography disrupted the thinking of even committed Northern Democrats like Hawthorne.

MARKETPLACE POLITICS

The scaffold scene in antislavery literature served many purposes. It drew attention to the fragility of the slave family and the complicity of the government in the commercial transaction threatening the family. The slave market also illustrated the doubly vulnerable position of the slave woman who was both deprived of citizenship rights and commercially valuable for her reproductive and sexual work. Countless stories and pictures showed slave traders tearing children from weeping slave mothers. And behind these brutes, abolitionists argued, was the federal government, which, at best, encouraged slavery through benign neglect. At its worst, the federal government actively promoted slave interests; slaves were frequently shown emerging from prison to underscore the state's role in upholding the private, "domestic" institution. Lydia Maria Child, for example, used the practice of storing slaves bound for auction in federal prisons as evidence of the federal government's non-neutrality on the issue of slavery: "But Washington is the great emporium of the internal slave-trade! The United States jail is a perfect storehouse for slave merchants . . . " (Appeal 33). Far from a sectional, domestic institution, slavery was a federally protected commercial institution.

Hester's emergence from prison at the opening of *The Scarlet Letter* and her painful journey to the marketplace scaffold strikingly resemble the trips of slaves depicted in antislavery literature. Hester's public exposure as a scarlet woman operates as a kind of sexual violation, making her sexual history available for public consumption. And like similar scenes in antislavery literature, Hester appears with her infant, prefiguring the vulnerability of the mother-child bond. Their appearance without a father and husband leads, as in the antislavery stories, to questions about the identity of the father and his responsibility to the mother and child.

The three scaffold scenes structuring the novel repair the family and restore Hester's social identity. Hester's first time on the scaffold is a democratic punishment, exactly equivalent to the accumulated scorn among the citizens witnessing her shame. After sentencing her to a short prison term and three hours on the scaffold, the magistrates defer to civil society, allowing the community to interpret her sin, identified by the scarlet A, however they wish. Should civil society consider her infraction a slight one, they will once again welcome her into the community. When Hester's society reaches a more severe consensus, each citizen individually refuses to recognize her as a fellow citizen. Her punishment stems not from the state, but from civil society. Inasmuch as Hester serves most of her prison sentence prior to the novel's opening, the plot is concerned with this civil punishment.

Hester, in turn, performs her penance through the operations of the marketplace, circulating with her sewing and her nursing through the private homes of those who previously judged her wicked. But for her trade and her nursing, she would have no opportunity to provoke her community's reconsideration of her status. Through her work, she is able to redefine herself according to the same market logic that originally fixed her punishment. She slowly gathers a new reputation among her individual patrons. The "invisible hand" of the market adjusts Hester's reputation, compensating her good behavior as her stigma comes to stand for "Able" (177) rather than "Adulteress." Hawthorne's Puritan market-place, as Sacvan Bercovitch persuasively argues, epitomizes a democratic civil society.

While such a reading accounts for the community's changing inter-pretation of Hester, it does not register the manipulation that is at the heart of *The Scarlet Letter*. In the open marketplace of meaning, the realm of Bercovitch's "liberal consensus," citizens with partial interpretations circulate, compromise, and trust in a utopia of future consensus. Lib-eral consensus, as Bercovitch describes it, is simply the sum of individual judgments circulating freely within a community. Nowhere in this theory of liberal consensus are there meaning-making institutions; silent, covert rebels; or tactics affecting people at a subconscious level, outside the realm of public discourse where old, rehearsed arguments could effectively inure the listener to even the most horrific stories.

Hester's journey from jail to scaffold provides a telling illustration of the way in which marketplace freedom disguises state protected tyranny. The state, in fact, conditions liberal consensus. As Bercovitch has shown, the office of the scarlet letter is to forestall the open rebellion that might jeopardize the community if disruptive views were not both acknowl-edged and tagged as the product of an "unruly individual." Bercovitch defines the operation of liberal consensus as a process that incorporates dissent by forestalling closure, that permits several "truths" to coexist until some "surer ground" can be established. The "office of the scarlet letter" is to marginalize Hester and at the same time to hold out the possibil-ity of her rejoining the community if she consents to its judgment of her—always provisional and always variable—symbolized by the "A" on her breast. The exact meaning of her scarlet letter, that is, the wages of her sin—and the slave's price—may be most visibly determined in the marketplace, but only after it is first institutionally gauged.

Hawthorne envisions civil society as more coercive—thus engendering more resistance—than Bercovitch's description of liberal consensus would suggest. Hester's careful manipulation of secret identities and her silent campaign for social recognition enable her to slowly alter her identity within the community and along with her identity the status of her child. She nurtures dissident impulses until such time when she can success-fully act upon them without losing custody of Pearl. She resolves after her second appearance on the scaffold, this time with Dimmesdale, to save the minister from his suffering by escaping from Salem with him. Hes-ter resists the community's conclusion that her affair with Dimmesdale was wrong. Without repenting, she nevertheless secures the reputation for being an appropriate advisor on romantic relations. Hester's resistance, while not as openly confrontational as Yellin hoped to find, does result in Hester's greater influence, without jeopardizing Pearl's welfare. Hester influences her community through her manipulation of public spectacle and private relationships much like abolitionists influenced the political and realm through their increasing presence in the literary and material marketplaces.[15] This cultural power allowed them to infiltrate private spaces, nurture a feminist consciousness, and achieve public power through indirect means.

The scaffold scenes do not entirely undercut the feminist subtext of the antislavery sign as Yellin suggests they do. The first scaffold scene ends with Hester's discovery of her husband in the crowd and her refusal to disclose the father of her child to the magistrates. Dreading Chillingworth's vengeance, she prefers the "shelter" of "these thousand witnesses" to a personal interview with him (69). While the narrator remarks that her features "should have been seen only in the quiet gleam of the fireside, in the happy shadow of a home, or beneath a matronly veil, at church," the unregulated violence of the private sphere for wife or slave could clearly be worse than the marketplace at noon.

Moreover, this happy domestic scene, repeatedly used in domestic fiction as an endorsement of "separate spheres," is revealed to be part of a coercive ideology. Later in the novel, when Hester is trying to dispel her resentment toward Chillingworth, she recalls "when he used to emerge at eventide from the seclusion of his study, and sit down in the firelight of their home and in the light of her nuptial smile" (193). But far from softening her feelings, the scene provokes disgust.

> She deemed it her crime most to be repented of that she had ever endured, and reciprocated, the lukewarm grasp of his hand, and had suffered the smile of her lips and eyes to melt into his own. And it seemed a fouler offense committed by Roger Chillingworth than any which had since been done him that, in the time when her heart knew no better, he had persuaded her to fancy herself happy by his side. (193)

Chillingworth, a middle-aged man, can only persuade Hester to accept the "marble image of happiness" rather than the "warm reality" because she is, unlike Chillingworth, an unworldly girl of genteel poverty (194). For Hawthorne's audience, such a girl was the ideal "angel in the home," other-centered, content with her domestic responsibilities, and untouched by public and commercial cultures. But in this passage, the angel in the home is nothing more than the happy slave, duped by a powerful ideology to accept a degrading role.

Hester not only flees "for refuge, as it were, to the public expo-sure" when she sees Chillingworth but she seeks refuge in the public eye throughout the next seven years. Hester's unwillingness to accept her neighbors' overtures once her good works are appreciated reveal her determination to embrace the symbol on her breast and make it a pub-lic sign not of her sin but of her opposition to the law that bound her to a man she did not love. "If they were resolute to accost her, she laid her finger on the scarlet letter, and passed on" (177). Hester intensifies her own isolation as a protest. She becomes more famous for her strength (A for Able) (177) than her social infraction (A for Adulteress).

Deprived of a citizen's power to directly address her community, Hes-ter engages in a subtle "public relations" campaign. Like those feminist abolitionists who rejected the public speaking platform but embraced the marketplace, Hester uses her commercial exposure and access to private spaces to sway townspeople toward reconsidering whether her crime was a sin and whether her daughter should inherit her outcast status. Hes-ter's approach is similar to that of Lydia Maria Child, who refused public speaking opportunities. Child sought to appeal to a broad range of read-ers during her editorship of the *National Anti-Slavery Standard*, which she turned into a "family newspaper" (Karcher 273). The literary marketplace offered access to the public, a forum for political commentary, with a kind of plausible deniability. Hester can be both self-effacing *and* convey a sub-tle message of resistance. Child could both claim to be a domestic woman, an expert on housewifery and children, *and* offer the public a critique of slavery's effect on the family. The marketplace offered women an oppor-tunity to redefine their roles and also to make a public spectacle of the domestic as a means of reforming it.

Hawthorne envied the special appeal women writers had in the mar-ketplace. He linked women writers to Ann Hutchinson in his sketch of the early Puritan and Hutchinson to Hester Prynne in *The Scarlet Letter*. Hawthorne believed that women writers of the nineteenth century—like Ann Hutchinson and Hester Prynne before them—enjoyed an erotic advantage over their male counterparts. Their writing was a "display of woman's naked mind to the gaze of the world" ("Mrs. Hutchinson" 2316). Furthermore, there were "obvious circumstances which will ren-der female pens more numerous and more prolific than those of men" (2315). Hawthorne probably believed that women authors were compar-atively free from financial worries, provided for by husbands or fathers and free to write prolifically. If so, Hawthorne's own financial worries dis-torted his view of his female contemporaries, many of whom struggled with the same conflicting goals as Hawthorne.[16]

Hester's secret affair holds the citizenry in suspense during the seven long years when she repeatedly appears before them in her capacity as noncitizen/producer. Among other motivations for buying Hester's sewing is the "morbid curiosity" of her customers (89). The antislavery family protection campaign worked on this level, producing both a sympathetic response and repulsion. Feminist abolitionists who became public speakers, such as Abby Kelley and the Grimke sisters, drew large audiences in part because of the "morbid curiosity" of listeners unaccustomed to women speakers. Similarly, their emotionally evocative products—sewing, gift books, commemorative coins—attracted and repulsed consumers. Hester's customers also try to secure a bit of her mystique by buying her sewing. The "fertility" and gorgeous luxuriance of her sewing, so expressive of her "Oriental nature," seem a part of Hester, unlike Hawthorne's Custom House work, which casts a "numbness" and "torpor" on him and makes his characters like "corpses." Where Hawthorne's name, circulating on goods passing through Salem, says little of his nature, Hester's works are symptoms of her sublimated passions. Hester is not made sterile by alienated labor. Her initial ignominy eventuates in her more widespread influence.

Michel de Certeau's distinction between hegemonic "strategy" and counter-hegemonic "tactics" sheds some light on Hester's restricted options for resistance.[17] Certeau defines strategy as the network of "force-relationships" developed between an institutional power with a distinct physical space (the space of "proper" conduct) and the institution's "environment," those without institutional power (XIX). Tactics, on the other hand, are the provisional, opportunistic actions of those who "play on and with a terrain . . . organized by the law of a foreign power" (37). Tactics are both visible to and dependent upon the power they would resist. To the extent that Hester takes the "color" of her life from the community's definition of the "A," whose terms have been initially established in the public marketplace of the theocracy, she becomes the disciplined subject of the Salem theocracy. She is on their terrain; her roots in their soil. But to the extent that she believes in a reunification with Dimmesdale beyond their grasp, or perhaps worse, a more saintlike purity despite the broken law, she is poised for resistance. Strategies are imposed through the domination of physical space, while tactical resistance occurs through the subtle manipulation of time. If the theocracy controls the space of the prison, the marketplace, and the church, Hester, over time, alters the significance of her scarlet letter.

In the chapters between the first and second scaffold scene, Hester not only reestablishes her access to the community, but wins her battle for custody of Pearl, a battle foreground by her appearance on the scaffold with her child. Further evidence of the icon's antislavery trace is that Hawthorne builds on its specific emotional resonance. Hester's opening scene prefigures the magistrates' discussion of separating Hester and Pearl in Chapter 7, a consideration Hawthorne divorces from its Puritan context. In seventeenth-century Puritan culture it was common to temporarily separate even very young children from their parents to ensure that they would be properly disciplined. But in *The Scarlet Letter* it appears as an extraordinary event caused by Hester's marked status in the community. Her mark and not her child's conduct provoke the move to separate the family. (It is right after Pearl's shocking denial of God as her Father that Dimmesdale talks the Governor out of taking Pearl away from Hester.)

Hester does not secure custody of Pearl because of her "mother's rights" but because she covertly threatens Dimmesdale:

> Speak thou for me! . . . Thou wast my pastor, and hadst charge of my soul, and knowest me better than these men can. I will not lose the child! Speak for me! Thou knowest—for thou has sympathies which these men lack!—thou knowest what is in my heart, and what are a mother's rights, and how much the stronger they are when that mother has but her child and the scarlet letter! Look thou to it! I will not lose the child! Look to it! (123)

Twice Hester demands that Dimmesdale speak for her, and twice she says "thou knowest." Despite her assertion of a "mother's rights," it is her specific hold over Dimmesdale, what both "know" about Dimmesdale's secret guilt, that ensures he will act as her advocate. If, as Bercovitch claims, the theocracy contains Hester's radical impulses (at least temporarily) through the public, visible sign that both isolates and exercises a disciplinary function over her thinking, she is adept, nonetheless, at manipulating the secrets and private spaces of Salem to forward her own agenda. In such a hostile environment, in which her enemies control the physical terrain, the "soil" in which she had struck her "roots" (86), Hester has only the daily repetition of her good works and the knowledge of hidden sins with which to exercise power. Hester secures custody of Pearl not because she has a right to the child and not because her overt arguments carry the day, but because she has power over Dimmesdale. As Leland S. Person notes, the scene at the Governor's Hall invokes "scenes of slave mothers begging for their maternal rights before intransigent slave owners, who had no legal obligation to care about the welfare of mothers or children." Hester's indirect tactics succeed; she never wins a confrontation through direct argument, and she would, indeed, likely lose Pearl in the attempt.

If, as Sacvan Bercovitch argues, *The Scarlet Letter* celebrated the isolation and eventual incorporation of resistance, we would expect Pearl's isolation to end with her incorporation into the Boston community. We would expect the "spell," which had left her "elements ... all in disorder," to be broken by some reconciliation between Pearl and her community (282, 98). No such reconciliation takes place. Pearl leaves Boston right after her father's public recognition in the third scaffold scene and does not return with Hester.

When Hester returns to Boston, she not only resumes her scarlet letter, but resumes her outpost in the woods, also refusing incorporation in the Puritan community. Bercovitch claims that Hester's return signals that she has acquiesced to the Puritan view of her affair with Dimmesdale. The case for this reading remains ambiguous, though. It is equally possible that she advises women in the tactics of resistance—public martyrdom and private manipulation. Our story, passing as it does from rumor to masculine, official culture (the Surveyors of the Customs) only tells us that Hester's cottage becomes a center for unhappy women, and Hester becomes an advisor. What does she counsel? The novel concludes by advancing only one option: she advises patience and quiet acceptance of the status quo. But in "The Custom House," Hawthorne imagines she "was looked upon by others as an intruder and a nuisance" (35). Just as Hester appeared to be penitent, even as she plotted to escape Salem with Dimmesdale, her female outpost on the margins of the town may have appeared more acquiescent than it was. The first seven years of humiliation and ostracism—with which the novel is almost exclusively concerned—had only hardened her resistance to marriage norms, leading her to plot an elopement with Dimmesdale. It seems unlikely that her sojourn in Europe without the scarlet letter would have succeeded where the first seven years failed.

What does Hawthorne's use of the scaffold trope say about the limitations and advantages of the family protection campaign? One limitation of the campaign was its ambivalent response to the marketplace. Part of the emotional resonance of slave market stories derived from domestic ideology that celebrated separate domestic and commercial spheres. According to this ideology, the domestic sphere had to be protected from the commercial sphere where competition and greed maximized production. Domestic ideology was premised on the idea that the domestic sphere was opposed to and superior to the commercial, governed by affection and cooperation between strong and weak family members. If, however, Hester's resistance to marriage norms and, in fact, the cultural campaign of the feminist abolitionists was disseminated through this "contaminated" sphere of the marketplace, then the message of the feminist abolitionists could indict their means.[18] If we sympathize with Hester as a martyr, then does she lose our sympathy when she ceases to be a victim, when her public exposure no longer seems a violation of her womanhood but an expression of her dissent, even her pride?

Feminist abolitionists did not, in fact, absolutely condemn the marketplace, only the way in which its "freedoms" disguised a very real tyranny. The federal government established some—men and slaveholders—as individuals with the right to make contracts. Others—wives and slaves—were specifically denied contract rights by virtue of their incorporation in the domestic. Equal access to contract rights offered women and African Americans the potential to reshape the domestic realm. Hester's freedom from marriage—Chillingworth chooses to keep his identity secret to wreak a covert revenge on his patient Dimmesdale—enables her access to the marketplace. Feminist abolitionists understood the marketplace, especially the literary marketplace, to be a more accessible sphere than the speaking podium or the political sphere.

By building on the values of the emerging middle class, the family protection campaign used a powerful wedge to convert some and render others mute on the issue of slavery. Caught between "feeling" and "principle," Hawthorne remained nearly silent on the moral principles challenging slavery. He sympathized, nonetheless, with oppressed African Americans and felt compelled by the courage and fortitude of reformers. His use of the slave market trope arouses the reader's sympathy for Hester. The reader stands in a position analogous to the young mother who admonishes the severe, bloodthirsty women around her: "Oh peace, neighbors, peace! . . . do not let her hear you! Not a stitch in that embroidered letter, but she felt it in her heart" (59). Hester is not, however, a shrinking, defeated woman in the tradition of the seduction tale; like the feminist abolitionists she is patterned after, her "haughty smile" and "unabashed" glance tell of the fortitude that would allow her to reemerge unrepentant on the marketplace scaffold at the novel's climax (57).[19] The family protection campaign successfully restructured the feelings Americans had toward slaves and the reformers, black and white, who braved public condemnation to stand with them.

CHAPTER 4

THE INVISIBLE HAND OF THE MARKETPLACE: E.D.E.N. SOUTHWORTH'S SOUTHERN REFORMS

Like Nathaniel Hawthorne, E.D.E.N. Southworth responded to the tropes of the antislavery campaign by imagining a heroine who defied conventional standards of feminine conduct by circulating in the free market. Both Hester and Capitola Black, the protagonist of Southworth's novel *The Hidden Hand; or, Capitola the Madcap* (1859), are cut off from family connections and forced to support themselves. Both carry signs, inscribed on their bodies, setting them apart from other women and suggesting a range of interpretive possibilities. Capitola's birthmark, a red "hidden hand" on the inside of her palm, identifies her as her mother's daughter and the heiress of a large fortune. But the birthmark also suggests an affinity for Adam Smith's theory of the market's "invisible hand," a tendency for individuals pursuing their own self-interest to collectively maximize the community's well-being. Pursuing her own self-interest, Capitola, like Smith's invisible hand, becomes an agent of positive social change. Contrary to the tenets of separate-spheres ideology, which predicted grave consequences to families and the nation should women enter the public sphere, Capitola's egoism and public adventures curb the excesses of the strong and promote the interests of the weak. All of her apparent transgressions ultimately result in the greater harmony of the community.

Lacking Hawthorne's ambivalence toward public women, Southworth created a character who unapologetically represents the independence and entrepreneurial spirit extolled in the emerging industrial capitalism of the mid-nineteenth century. Capitola empowers herself by manipulating public spectacle and deflecting patriarchal criticisms with humor and irony. As an antislavery Southerner, Southworth represents Northern "free labor" as a positive alternative—especially for white women—to the organic culture of the Southern plantation.

While Southworth was not a central figure in either the abolitionist or feminist movements, she popularized a view of North and South, of free labor and slave labor, and of the gender roles available in these economic systems that exemplify the strengths and weaknesses of the uneasy alliance between feminism and antiracism. The most significant antislavery feminists made enormous financial sacrifices and became social pariahs to lead the movement. Southworth is distinctive because she used the antislavery press as a stepping stone into literary fame. She became the country's most popular female novelist of the antebellum South by learning how to play into emerging discourse on race and gender without inspiring the public revolt that even a talented propagandaist like Lydia Maria Child did. This chapter will consider *The Hidden Hand* in the context of Southworth's other antebellum novels and in the context of antislavery literature to illustrate the potential and limits of the period's discourse on race and gender.

Southworth was the prolific author of at least 60 novels and eight collections of short stories (Dobson and Hudock 287). Her works were extraordinarily popular during her writing life, between 1846 and 1899, and they were read in Europe as well as the United States. She grew up in Washington, D.C., and frequently visited her mother's family in the wooded areas of Maryland and Virginia, where she set many of her novels. She and her sister were often excluded from their stepfather's company, and they spent much time with the family's slaves. When she married, she moved west with her husband, returning to Washington, D.C., pregnant, with a young son, and without her husband four years later. Little is known of what happened in the marriage, though her husband apparently abandoned the family, and Southworth turned to teaching and writing to support her children.

The Hidden Hand was Southworth's most popular novel, appearing in serialized form in the *New York Ledger* in 1859, 1868–1869, and again in 1883 (291). Robert Bonner, the editor of the nonpartisan *Ledger*, boasted that one-eighth of the population of the United States read his weekly paper. He attributed its success, in part, to the "universally popular authoress" E.D.E.N. Southworth with whom he had an exclusive contract (qtd. in Looby 197). Many enjoyed seeing dramatic adaptations of the *The Hidden Hand* in the United States and England, and when the novel emerged as a book in 1888, it became a best seller (Habegger 199).

SOUTHWORTH AS ANTISLAVERY WRITER

Southworth has long been known as an antislavery writer, and until recently, *The Hidden Hand* was considered an antislavery text. Certainly, Southworth emerged from an antislavery milieu. Close personal friends included John Greenleaf Whittier and Harriet Beecher Stowe, the author of the blockbuster *Uncle Tom's Cabin*. Whittier, in fact, encouraged the editor of *The National Era*, an abolitionist paper, to give Southworth her start (Boyle 8, 15). *The National Era* published *Retribution*, her first novel, in 1849. In many ways *Retribution* conformed to the antislavery narratives circulating at the time. It celebrated the generosity of a white heroine, Hester Dent, who attempted to free her slaves, and featured a tragic mulatta, a biracial, Cuban woman whose white father neglects to free her before his death. Southworth clearly drew upon antislavery literary conventions in this novel. Cementing her reputation as an antislavery writer, Southworth allowed her home in Washington, D.C., to be used as a reserve hospital during the Civil War, and she housed President Lincoln for three nights as he traveled on war business (15).

Recent critics, however, most especially Christopher Looby, have cast doubt on the conventional wisdom that *The Hidden Hand* was an antislavery novel. Looby distinguishes between the publishing history of *Retribution* and *The Hidden Hand*, noting that *The Hidden Hand* was serialized in the nonpartisan, enormously successful paper *Ledger*, where it attracted Southern as well as Northern readers with its minstrel stereotypes, its "irascible old master," and its "skittishly evasive but loyal slave" (198).

Looby is absolutely right in his critique of the racial politics of *The Hidden Hand*; nonetheless, the novel does not mark a departure from Southworth's earlier novel *Retribution*, a book that critics, including Looby, agree is an antislavery novel. Both texts feature negative black stereotypes and both appropriate the dilemmas faced by these black characters to dramatize the more central dilemmas faced by the white heroines. For example, *Retribution* features a tragic mulatta who is negatively stereotyped as having "very feeble intellect" and "very strong feelings," a combination requiring "the restraining and governing influences of religious culture" (Southworth, *Retribution* 40).

Even more significantly, the focus of *Retribution* is not upon the injustices of slavery, which are hardly depicted and then are deflected onto distant Cuba. Instead, the novel follows Ernest Dent, a much admired abolitionist, who "oppresse[s]" and "deceive[s]" his wife (143). Ernest marries his ward, Hester, seemingly to assure that she will free her slaves once she reaches 21 and to extend his experiment in paying wages to slaves. This experiment is announced early in the novel but never directly shown. Ernest's oppression consists of demanding an extreme form of self-effacement; he incessantly reprimands Hester. The humble Hester at one point asks herself, "When shall I ever merit this lofty man's esteem?" (39). Ultimately, he deceives her by falling in love with her best friend, a beautiful social climber.

A clear parallel exists in the novel between Hester's slaves and Hester herself, both of whom are oppressed, deceived, and betrayed by their legal guardians. The slaves expect Hester and Ernest to free them, a plan frustrated by Hester's death just hours before her twenty-first birthday. Her death is allegedly hastened by her husband's neglect so that the abolitionist is responsible, ironically, for both his wife's early death and the prolonged captivity of her slaves. The "retribution" of the title refers to Ernest's punishment for his wife's oppression and not, as one of the *National Era's* readers might suppose, to any retribution slave owners or traders might face. The novel ends with an extended consideration of Ernest's humiliation at the hands of his second wife—a siren who cuckolds him. The slaves on Hester's plantation are freed on the last page of the novel, an event of little interest but for the hardship this sacrifice causes Hester's brave and generous daughter. Hester's slaves are not a central concern of the novel nor of the ironically named abolitionist Ernest.

While the racial politics of the two novels are similar, they differ dramatically in their style and resolution: *Retribution* is written firmly within the sentimental tradition, and it fails to point toward an alternative social organization that would resolve the fundamental forces distorting and limiting the lives of the novel's white, female characters. In fact, when Hester's daughter frees her slaves, she is described as impoverished and disempowered. In contrast, *The Hidden Hand* rejects sentimentality and offers Northern entrepreneurial capitalism as the institutional solution to women's oppression in the South.

Southworth does not tame her abolitionism in *The Hidden Hand* for the *Ledger*. On the contrary, her particular form of abolition finds its fullest expression in *The Hidden Hand* where she develops her critique of the South's organic culture. In both novels, her objection to the slave South revolves around the treatment of white women and the role of the family in public life rather than the exploitation and abuse of slaves. This makes her atypical among feminist abolitionists who usually were devoted to a thorough unveiling of the brutality faced by slaves. Southworth's Capitola operates as a female avenger, liberating the other white women in the text from their dispossession and marginalization in the South's organic culture.

SENTIMENTALITY, FEMALE MASOCHISM, AND THE SOUTH'S ORGANIC CULTURE

Organic societies imagine the state to be a macrocosm of the family, with a benevolent father figure governing, with sympathy and firmness, the subordinates who owe him obedience. The term "organic" comes from John Winthrop's comparison between the ideal state and the human body. In his best-known political speech, "A Modell of Christian Charity" (1630), Winthrop laid out a blueprint for how Puritans making the arduous journey to New England ought to relate to one another in the new settlement. The health of the whole, he argued, depended upon the health of each part, just as in the body. Moreover, depending so entirely upon one another in the new settlement, the settlers were bound to feel a "sensibleness and sympathy" for one another (Winthrop). This "sympathy" was crucial because it meant that each part would willingly sacrifice, without conscious consideration, for the good of the whole. Moreover, individual parts played different roles: some people permanently filled more exalted roles than others; some were heads and some feet.

Melvin Yazawa associates organic culture with the colonial period in American history. After the Revolution, according to Yazawa, the state was viewed more as a machine than a family or a body, and citizens bore an individual allegiance to that egalitarian, depersonalized machine. I would argue, however, that this process did not proceed uniformly throughout the United States. Southern agrarians, including contemporaries of Southworth's, still promoted a familial paradigm as the Southern ideal into the twentieth century.[1] George Fitzhugh, for example, bemoaned the advent of "free laborers" who were nothing more than "slaves without masters." In his 1857 essay, "Southern Thought," he wrote, "[T]he poor have been turned over from the parental and protective rule of kings, barons, and churchmen, to the unfeeling despotism of capitalists, employers, usurers, and extortioners [sic]; and this was called emancipation!" (2008). Celebrated in Southern journals, organic culture was troubling to many feminist abolitionists who were just developing a language and sign system for representing and critiquing it. Women, children, and slaves in the familial model were doubly subordinated insofar as the father figure's private power in the family extended into the public sphere. He was responsible for the behavior of his subordinates and could, with little interference, use the powers of the state to punish his family dependents. In the South, where this model still prevailed, slaves could be whipped by public authorities or women sent to insane asylums at the will of patriarchs and without trial or public notice.

Living most of her life in Washington, D.C., Southworth set the majority of her family dramas on plantations and explored the circumscribed lives of white women who did not enjoy the protections promised in an organic culture. With titles such as *The Deserted Wife, The Discarded Daughter, The Lost Heiress, The Missing Bride, The Unloved Wife*, and *The Rejected Bride*, Southworth's novels often prescribed patience and faithful resignation. Women's empowerment rested upon their ability to subdue any form of ego and to have their extreme renunciations ultimately discovered and admired by those with power. These novels sought to restore women's protected position within the family rather than help them to achieve any enduring public power. Hester Dent in *Retribution* is but one example of this type of heroine who invokes sentimental identification from the reader and public censure of tyrannical husbands in order to make the community safe for women to return to the private sphere.[2]

This lesson in masochistic power is, perhaps, most clearly taught in Southworth's 1853 short story "The Better Way: Or, the Wife's Victory." It is the companion piece to "The Married Shrew," which records Southworth's idea of the *wrong* way to resist husbands, by berating them and neglecting domestic duties in favor of worldly recognition. Mary Leslie submits to her husband even when he insists she relinquish custody of her beloved daughter to a wealthy relative. Ultimately, Mary is "victorious" because her absolute obedience and her intense suffering cause her husband to have a change of heart:

> Unknown to Mary, there was one spectator to this scene. Leslie was standing within the door. He had entered, silently and unobserved, at the moment that Mary had lain the sleeping Sylvia on the bed, and sunk down by her side in prayer. The first words of the prayer arrested his intention of coming forward or speaking. He had seen, and had heard—and never before had the pure and holy heart of his wife been so unveiled as in that prayer; and while it yet ascended, in all its Christian beauty and eloquence, he quietly withdrew from the room, murmuring, "The angel, the angel, how blind I have been!"

Crucial to the efficacy of this scene is Mary's unawareness that she is observed. She is no actress and has not choreographed the scene. Her suffering is punctuated by Leslie's initial coldness and imperious demands on her. His power and sadism are part of his attraction; he offers Mary the opportunity to ecstatically suffer, perfect her martyrdom, and achieve the status of "angel."[3] Like Hester, Mary transforms her powerful husband through her extreme suffering, making him devoted to her and to her interests. He severely reprimands her when she tries direct advocacy but reveres her self-denying sacrifices.

Capitola stands out among Southworth's heroines for her rejection of the masochistic form of power Southworth's other antebellum heroines embraced. *The Hidden Hand* tells the story of Capitola, a wealthy, Southern heiress whose evil uncle, Gabriel Le Noir, has killed her father and has hidden her pregnant mother in the attic of the family mansion in order to steal the family fortune. Just after Capitola's birth the mother implores the midwife—a light-skinned, free black woman named Nancy Grewell—to escape with the infant. Gabriel Le Noir hires an outlaw to kill the child, but instead the outlaw abducts Nancy Grewell and Capitola, turning them over to a slave trader. The two escape to New York and live as fugitives. On a clandestine trip to Virginia to tell her story to the local magistrate, Major Warfield, Nancy Grewell dies, leaving Warfield the only character who knows Capitola's parentage.

Left in New York, Capitola finds herself, like many a street child, without parents or guardians. Initially, the 12-year-old responds as the typical sentimental heroine, retreating to her last home, hoping for some external intervention, and searching, unsuccessfully, for work as a seamstress. Capitola changes her approach to poverty, however, when a wrecking ball destroys her home, symbolizing the end of her sentimental martyrdom and her reliance on romantic interventions. From here forward the novel becomes what Joanne Dobson has dubbed "a peculiarly inverted sentimental novel" and what Carol Lauhon calls "a national capitalist epic" featuring a female Horatio Alger ("The Hidden Hand: Subversion" 232; 11). Feisty Capitola dons boys' clothes and becomes a newsboy in the toughest section of New York, the Bowery. The aptly named Capitola succeeds admirably in the free market, parlaying her quick tongue, chutzpah, and good looks into many odd jobs. For 18 months she supports herself in this manner until her identity as a girl is revealed and she is brought before a court for her impersonation.[4] Anticipating later Horatio Alger narratives, Southworth rewards Capitola's honesty and hard work with a generous patron, Major Warfield, who has traveled to New York to find the heiress. When he intercedes to protect the unknown girl, he discovers that he has coincidentally found his heiress. He offers to adopt her and take her to Virginia but does not tell Capitola of her true identity.

Throughout the novel, Southworth uses a series of more conventional female characters as counterpoints to the remarkable Capitola. It is this tension between the passive, martyred women and Capitola that drives the narrative forward as Capitola travels South, rectifying the injustices done to women in Southern slave society.

STAGING THE SELF: CAPITOLA AS PUBLIC WOMAN

The Hidden Hand is distinctive in Southworth's oeuvre for two reasons: it features a heroine who will not sacrifice her self-interest to please others, and it explicitly contrasts North and South. Most of Southworth's novels are set in Maryland and Virginia (Boyle 75); while other regions are alluded to, they are not commonly depicted in any significant detail. In *The Hidden Hand*, however, Capitola grows up in New York City. Her character is a Northern, urban product, and her strategies for self-determination form a glaring contrast with the strategies of the other women she meets in the South.

Capitola dramatizes the entrepreneurial ethos of the North when she explains, to Major Warfield's shock and disapproval, her transformation from a penniless girl into a newsboy with capital. She addresses him along with a crowd of bystanders as she is brought up on charges of impersonating a boy:

> "Well! Not to tire your honors, I went into that little back parlor a girl, and I came out a boy, with a suit of pants and jacket, with my hair cut short and a cap on my head! The pawnbroker gave me a penny roll and a six-pence for my black ringlets."
>
> "All seemed grist that came to his mill!" said [Major Warfield].
>
> "Yes, Governor, he was a dealer in general. Well, the first thing I did was to hire myself to him, at a sixpence a day, [...] to shovel in his coal. That didn't take me but a day. So at night he paid me, and I slept in peace behind a stack of boxes. Next morning I was up before the sun, and down to the office of the little penny paper, the 'Morning Star.' I bought two dozen of 'em, and ran as fast as I could to the ferry-boats to sell to the early passengers. Well, sir, in an hour's time I had sold out, and pocketed just two shillings, and felt myself on the high road to fortune!" (46–7)

Major Warfield considers the pawnbroker a shameless exploiter, but Capitola hears none of the disapproval. Being exempted from the marketplace as a girl is no honor to Capitola, who is proud that she, too, becomes a capitalist by donning a cap.[5] At the least, the marketplace allows Capitola safety and sustenance. But it also frees her to define herself as capable and charismatic. She charms Major Warfield with her brash newsboy speech and proudly tells the magistrates about her successes as a newsboy. By circulating in the marketplace, she meets people later helpful to her, including Major Warfield. The impersonality of the marketplace permits self-fashioning not possible in rural areas.

Traveling South with her new guardian, Capitola routinely breaks the very precepts celebrated in much of Southworth's other works. Hester

Dent and Mary Leslie win the narrator's regard, and at times their husbands', with their blind faith in their husbands' character. They never defy their husbands. Capitola routinely defies her guardian, Major Warfield. She rides after dark and to dangerous places; she exchanges epithets with him; she refuses his gifts. She analyzes and rejects the very dynamics Southworth's other heroines accept without questioning. Capitola inveighs against Major Warfield after he has insulted and upbraided her for one of her dangerous rides: "But, uncle, there is a sin that is worse, or at least more ungenerous, than ingratitude! It is to put a helpless fellow creature under heavy obligations, and then treat that grateful creature with undeserved contempt and cruel unkindness!" (123). Just to be sure that he understands she values respect over chivalry, she warns, "I vow I'll go back to Rag Alley, for a very little more! Freedom and peace are even sweeter than wealth and honors!" (124).

Capitola will accept nothing less than egalitarian treatment, and she parodies Major Warfield to drive home that point. Warfield chastises Capitola, saying, "Miss!! How dare you have the impudence to face me, much less the—the—the assurance!—the effrontery!—the audacity! The *brass* to speak to me!" (120). When Capitola tries to deflect his anger, he addresses her, "YOUNG WOMAN! Tell me instantly, and without prevarication where you have been?" (120). Capitola mimics his outburst a few days later when he returns from a trip: "Sir, how dare you the impudence to *face* me, much less the —the—the—the brass! the *bronze*! the COPPER! to speak to me?". When Major Warfield responds in bewilderment, she cinches the parody, "OLD GENTLEMAN, tell me instantly, and without prevarication, where have you been? (127)(see figure 4.1)."

Unlike Hester Dent, Mary Leslie, and an assortment of heroines from Southworth's other novels, Capitola is adept at winning the respect and favor of her guardian while still resisting subordination. She does not merely contradict him, thereby sacrificing her position in the family and wider community. She uses a host of strategies, including humor, parody, and staged scenes to have her cake and eat it, too. This is perhaps best illustrated by comparing Capitola to the other female characters in the novel.

Marah Rocke resembles many of Southworth's heroines in her victimization at the hands of her older, more powerful husband, who prevails upon her to enter into a secret marriage. As a teenager Marah falls in love with Major Warfield, then a man in his 40s, and secretly marries him while he is in camp with the army. He believes keeping their marriage secret will protect her from unwanted attention in the military, and he stows her away in a cabin some distance from the military camp. On the contrary, she becomes infamous among the men as the major's "pretty little favorite," and men begin to circle her home. Such secret marriages are the animating forces behind two of Southworth's other pre–Civil War novels,[6] and they closely resemble the familiar plotline of the tragic mulatta insofar as these women are isolated and entirely dependent on their husbands for their social status. When they are denied as wives, they find themselves in social free-fall. They become known as fallen women, and they and their children face exile and even starvation.

Major Warfield disowns her because Gabriel Le Noir sets a scene intended to convince the Major he is having an affair with Marah. For her part, Marah refuses to force the Major to support her and their son by appealing to the law. Marah accepts her banishment, becoming another of Southworth's female martyrs.

Capitola is expert at reversing these handicaps. She sets scenes designed to entrap her foes, and she manipulates the law to reenforce the public sentiment she's shaped. Perhaps the best example of this is when Gabriel Le Noir's son, Craven, attempts to force his father's ward, the heiress Clara, into marriage. Capitola switches costumes with Clara and encourages Clara to "swagger." She explicitly rejects the female masochism celebrated in sentimentality, saying, "If you go doing the sentimental you won't look like me a bit" (308). An antisentimental heroine, Capitola does not eschew public spectacle like Marah Rocke or Mary Leslie. On the contrary, Capitola proceeds to the church under a veil with Craven Le Noir, pretending to be Clara. The Le Noirs plan to have the marriage performed in an empty chapel, but there are several farm laborers quietly praying. The sight of these witnesses fills Cap's heart "with joy and exultation inasmuch as it ensured her final safety" (315). She "abandon[s] herself to the spirit of frolic" and creates a show to embarrass the Le Noirs and free Clara from their guardianship. When she declares she will not take Craven Le Noir as her husband and throws off her veil, the men ask the meaning of her performance. She replies, "It means the game's up, the play's over, villainy is about to be hanged, and virtue about to be rewarded, and the curtain is going to drop, and the principal performer—that's I—is going to be called out amid the applause of the audience!" (316).

Cap unabashedly creates a spectacle to illuminate truth, not as "artifice" was generally understood, to create a false impression. She goes on to claim the protection of the others in the church, to expose the plot of the Le Noirs, and to lay the groundwork to have their guardianship nullified. She enjoys the humorous play, but she does not enjoy telling Clara's tragic, conventionally sentimental tale: "And now, Herbert, let the two poor wretches go hide their mortification, and do you take me home, for I am immensely tired of doing the sentimental, making speeches, and piling up the agonies" (318). "Doing the sentimental" confers vicarious power; the weak claim the pity and protection of the strong, and they must earn this without directly asking for it as the many inadvertently glimpsed scenes of women's suffering demonstrate. Capitola seizes direct power by openly orchestrating scenes.

She again uses the public sphere to right the wrongs of an organic society when she defends her honor by staging a duel. She upends the dynamics of sentimental power, in which women's power is exercised vicariously through stronger men. Whereas sentimental heroines suffer beautifully and privately, are accidentally discovered in their martyrdom, and then vindicated by a man who can operate in the public realm, Capitola rejects martyrdom and vicarious power. When Craven Le Noir impugns her reputation, she reprimands her kinsman for failing to defend her honor (see figure 4.1). She haughtily mounts her horse, waylays Craven in the woods, and challenges him to a duel. Loading the pistols with dried peas, she fools Craven into thinking he has been shot. Afraid of dying unregenerate, he confesses his life of knavery to the magistrate, after which Capitola reveals his true, mildly wounded state. She gathers an audience for his confession by leading the neighbors to believe that the magistrate will shortly arrest her for Craven's murder.

Capitola uses and enlarges the public sphere with her pranks. Upset at the risks Capitola takes, Major Warfield has the following interchange with her:

> "Demmy, you New York newsboy, will you never be a woman? Why the demon didn't you tell *me*, sirrah? I would have called the fellow out and chastised him to your heart's consent. Hang it, Miss, answer me and say."
>
> "Because you are on the invalid list and I am in sound condition and capable of taking my own part," said Cap.
>
> "Then, answer me this: while you were taking your own part, why the foul fiend didn't you pepper him with something sharper than dried peas?"
>
> "I think he is quite as severely punished in suffering from extreme terror and intense mortification and public ridicule," said Cap. (376)

Unlike Marah Rocke, she does not defer to her male relatives to defend her reputation, and she refuses to lead a cloistered life that might be above reproach. She manipulates reputations like commodities in the market; their values are no longer fixed through marriage and family lineage, but they fluctuate through public exposure and advertisement. When Gabriel Le Noir ruins Marah Rocke, Marah eschews public appeal to reclaim her reputation, but Capitola exposes Craven by tricking him into a very public confession. Major Warfield intuitively recognizes this as a Northern, capitalist strategy; Capitola is not just acting in a masculine way, but as the

Figure 4.1 Both of these sketches appeared in 1859 when *The Hidden Hand* was first serialized in the *New York Ledger*. The top one shows Capitola reprimanding Wargrave, while in the lower one Capitola scolds a lazy cousin and vows to duel Craven LeNoir herself.

entrepreneurial newsboy. She does not need to damage Craven physically to hurt his marketplace value.

Capitola's mother, also named Capitola, is perhaps Southworth's best illustration of the danger of the organic society to women. A young, immigrant bride from France, she is whisked away from her Southern home just after giving birth to Capitola, heiress to the Le Noir fortune. Seemingly without inspiring any serious investigation, Gabriel Le Noir sends his sister-in-law to a mental asylum. Capitola compares the silence surrounding her disappearance with the publicity surrounding the disappearance of a Northern murder victim:

> "*Disappearance* did you say? Can a lady of condition disappear from a neighborhood and no inquiry be made for her?"
>
> "No, my dear, there was inquiry, and it was answered plausibly that Madame Eugene was insane and sent off to a lunatic asylum; but there are those who believe that the lovely lady was privately made way with," whispered Mrs. Condiment.
>
> "How dreadful! I did not think such things happened in a quiet country neighborhood. Something like that occurred, indeed, in New York, within my own recollection, however," said Capitola—who straightway commended and related the story of Mary Rogers, and all other stories of terror that memory supplied her with. (191)

Southworth refers here to a real woman, Mary Rogers, who became a media sensation when in 1841 "the beautiful cigar girl" of New York City disappeared and later washed up on the banks of the Hudson River. Newspapers followed the story daily, ferreting out dozens of witnesses to the woman's last days, though the case was never solved. The aspect of Madame Eugene's disappearance that most astonishes Capitola is the secrecy surrounding it; no one is willing to confront Gabriel Le Noir in his power to dispose of his dependents. Lydia Maria Child and Frederick Douglass, in describing Southern plantations, often emphasized their exemption from the public gaze, which gave extraordinary power to the patriarch. In one story, Child compared a plantation's isolation to a "seclusion, almost as deep as that of the oriental harem" ("Slavery's Pleasant Homes" 239). Douglass more explicitly discussed the dangers of this extremely truncated public sphere: "Public opinion is, indeed, an unfailing restraint upon the cruelty and barbarity of masters, overseers, and slave-drivers, whenever and wherever it can reach them; but there are certain secluded and out-of-the-way places, even in the state of Maryland, seldom visited by a single ray of healthy public sentiment—where slavery, wrapt [*sic*] in its own congenial, midnight darkness, can, and does,

develop all its malign and shocking characteristics; where it can be inde-
cent without shame, cruel without shuddering, and murderous without
apprehension or fear of exposure" (*My Bondage* 44).

Veronica Stewart rightly links the novel's preoccupation with secrecy
and seclusion to conventional romance plots. She argues that "Le Noir's
stratagems demonstrate that corrupt men can manipulate existing laws
and social mores to their own purposes with relative ease" (157). Capitola,
Stewart shows, is constructed as the antidote to such sentimental plots;
she refuses to "do the sentimental" as she tells Clara. Unlike the typical
romance novel, Southworth's novel does not depict the law as the means
by which the hero or heroine can achieve recognition and vindication.
Stewart insists, "Although the text showboats Capitola's lawlessness, every
woman character in *The Hidden Hand* functions (in varying degrees and
fashions) outside the law" (160).

Stewart's argument, however, does not take Capitola's interactions with
the courts into account. The novel does project forward to a time when
the legal system might more justly represent the interests of women.
Capitola's exploits three times end with a publicity campaign forcing the
legal institutions to reverse earlier judgments. Clara Day wins freedom
from Gabriel Le Noir's guardianship once Capitola exposes his nefarious
plot to force Clara to marry his son. Craven is left in the magistrate's
hands after Capitola inveigles a confession from him that also frees her
from an attempted murder charge. Capitola's mother wins freedom from
the insane asylum once she has the testimony of Capitola's friend Tra-
verse, a doctor. Capitola uses parody and public performance to make
the legal system represent women's interests. Capitola's frequent correc-
tion of Major Warfield, himself a magistrate, and the courts of law align
her with Lydia Maria Child in the project of making the law better represent the interests of women and children. Southworth indicts a legal
system (coverture)[7] that does not give white women independent standing in contracts or in court, but she does not imagine African Americans
enjoying a similar legal presence, despite her reputation for antislavery
commitments.

BORROWING FROM THE BOWERY B'HOY AND MINSTRELSY

Southworth signals the connection between white women's fates and
slaves in the South in several ways. Most obviously, the proliferation
of the names Black, Le Noir, and Raven serve to connect black and
white characters throughout the novel. Also, Capitola is briefly con-
signed to slavery with the light-skinned African American midwife Nancy
Grewell. The story of light-skinned women and children betrayed by
their guardians and fleeing slavery was a standard antislavery narrative.

Capitola's mysterious birth to unknown parents provokes readers' suspicions about her racial status until Major Warfield, nearly half way through the novel, reveals her parentage. Southworth invokes antislavery iconography to dramatize the disempowerment of white women and children, but this becomes an act of appropriation rather than an alliance helpful to African Americans.

The convergence of Capitola's life story and Nancy Grewell's serves to point out the very different roles played by black and white characters in Southworth. Nancy Grewell dies immediately after relating Capitola's story to the Major, and when Capitola hears of her foster mother's demise, she seems barely affected. Nancy Grewell is merely the device for introducing Southworth's heroine, a midwife in two senses. Moreover, when Capitola is introduced to her maid in Virginia, Pitapat, she remarks upon the similarities in their names: "Come, as I've got a 'pit' in my name and you've got a 'pit' in yours, we'll see if we two can't make something of this third pit" (76). But this bond is invoked only to point up the contrast between the two as Pitapat withdraws in fear and Capitola seizes her candle and investigates the trap door in her room. The narrator explains, "But this only made the horrible darkness 'visible'; no object caught or reflected a single ray of light—all was black, hollow, void and silent" (76). Capitola's relationship with Pitapat, "the poor little darkey," results not in an alliance but in a contrast that illuminates Capitola's heroism and makes "visible" Pitapat's difference (76). Pitapat lacks a narrative in the novel; neither her situation nor her character develop, and she fades from view before the end of the novel.

Capitola's last name, Black, initially suggests her affinity with slaves and her marginalization in her new Southern home. She repeatedly must defend her right to move freely outside of the domestic space and to speak publicly. Michelle Ann Abate astutely describes Capitola's performance as a "minstrelized form of gender rebellion" and points to her many scenes with the minstrel figures of Wool and Pitapat as evidence of her adaptation of their physical and verbal audacity (56). Abate goes on to argue,

> Although white tomboys and blackface minstrels are not commonly viewed or studied in tandem, they are twinned figures in many ways. Similarly interested in lampooning traditional gender roles, satirizing established codes of sexual conduct, and ridiculing conventional manners and mores, they perform much of the same cultural work. (57)

Like the minstrel shows of the period, the tomboy performance of Capitola achieves greater cultural power by permitting her the freedom from gender conventions and iconoclasm popularly accorded to African

Americans. Nonetheless, Southworth foregrounds Capitola's distance from African Americans. Abate remarks,

> Recalling the rhetorical strategy of many antebellum feminists who used the language of black slavery to characterize the condition of white womanhood, Cap repeatedly insists that she is not a "cur" or "slave" who will submit to the "gilded slavery" of patriarchal oppression. (58)

In the novel, Cap appropriates the rhetoric of antislavery to advance her own interests, often at the expense of her apparent allies, Wool and Pitapat.

In this respect, the stage versions of *The Hidden Hand* actually prove to be more daring than the novel itself. When Robert Jones adapted the novel to stage, he enlarged upon the minstrel scenes in the novel, and advertisements for the plays featured Wool as a major character played by some of the era's most famous performers, including F.S. Chanfrau. Chanfrau was most famous for portraying the beloved figure of Mose, the Bowery B'hoy, a bold, vernacular-speaking fireman who challenges the power of genteel, propertied men from the position of ethnic other (see figure 4.2). His version of Wool gave Wool more scenes in which he deliberately mocks and undermines Wargrave, emphasizing his alignment with Capitola in challenging Wargrave's power.[8] Chanfrau was a working-class hero, and he made Wool more than a minstrel character; he became truly confrontational and deliberate in his antics. At the end of Jones' play, Wool and Pitapat marry, giving them a much-enhanced status in the play.

Capitola exchanges her last name, "Black," for Greyson when she marries Northerner Herbert Greyson, a sailor and military hero. It's tempting to read this name change as a sacrifice of the gender bending implicit in both minstrelsy and tomboy behavior, as indeed Abate does, but the terms of her marriage to Greyson suggest a much different reading. Greyson represents a different sort of masculine hero, one who combines bravery and strength with a self-effacing blandness that leaves Capitola in control of the narrative. Grey suggests a balance of power, a mixing of assertiveness and respect for the autonomy of others. Alfred Habegger goes so far as to call Greyson a "milksop," "neuter," and "pantywaist" (208). Admittedly, there are no sexually charged scenes between the pair, but the seeds are sewn here for the companionate marriage trumpeted by early twentieth-century feminists. In one telling scene, Greyson physically restrains Craven Le Noir so that Capitola can give her soliloquy exposing Le Noir's evil machinations. Clearly, Greyson plays only a supporting role to Capitola's star position. Significantly, when Greyson proposes to Capitola, Wargrave remarks, "If I were to

"I'M BOUND NOT TO RUN WID DER MACHINE ANY MORE."
F.S. CHANFRAU IN THE CHARACTER OF "MOSE"
As originally written for and performed by him at the Olympic and Chatham Theatres, New York.
Lith & Published by E & J Brown 116 Fulton St N.Y.

Figure 4.2 F.S. Chanfrau became famous for depicting Mose, the Bowery B'hoy, a pugnacious and proud Irish fireman. He went on to star in the stage version of *The Hidden Hand*, playing Wool. Courtesy of the Harry T. Peters, "America on Stone" Lithography Collection, National Museum of American History, Behring Center, Smithsonian Institution.

object, you'd get married all the same! Demmy! You're both of age. Do as you please" (472). Wargrave does not consider Capitola his possession, and her anticipated union leaves her free to continue to perform in public.

Capitola becomes an antisentimental heroine by borrowing from both black-faced minstrelsy and the conventions of the Bowery b'hoy, both cultural forms enjoying great popularity in the industrializing North. Cap's ability to code-switch, to easily move between the b'hoy dialect and a more genteel one, to romp like a minstrel character and comport herself as a "lady," enables her to provoke questions about the conventional roles of women in an organic culture. The similarity between white women's and African Americans' positions in the organic culture of the South is asserted through Capitola's name and behavior, while simultaneously Southworth uses the African American characters as foils to show the white women's potential to emerge from the role of subordinate and martyr. Capitola advanced an alternative model of female identity and marriage that captivated many readers and theater patrons.

SINKING THE SOUTHERN ROMANCE IN PRINT AND ON STAGE

Writing after the South's defeat in the Civil War and the failures of Reconstruction, Samuel Clemens in *Huck Finn* famously sinks a boat on the Mississippi River, a boat inauspiciously named *Sir Walter Scott* for the Scottish writer credited with inspiring the Southern romance, replete with chivalric heroes, fratricidal hostilities, ardent heroes sacrificed in noble causes, and marriages that magically heal national tensions. With the inglorious sinking of *Sir Walter Scott*, Twain signals his efforts to sink the Southern romance once and for all. He attacks the Southern, extralegal code of honor and parodies tears and sentimentality. In *Life on the Mississippi*, Clemens blames Scott for "the debilitating influence of his books. Admiration of his fantastic heroes and their grotesque 'chivalry' doings and romantic juvenilities still survives here[in the South] . . .; and traces of its [*sic*] inflated language and other windy humbuggeries survive along with it [*sic*]" (195). The Southern romance, Twain suggests, is inherently dishonest and had disastrously led the South into a Quixotic, avoidable war.

In this one exceptional work, E.D.E.N. Southworth similarly criticizes the South and the Southern romance, forcefully demonstrating that "doing the sentimental"—understood in Southworth to entail female masochism—reinforces women's subordination in an organic culture. This may be difficult to reconcile with Southworth's devotion to the sentimental romance both before and after *The Hidden Hand*, but Southworth herself notes the unusual conditions under which she wrote the novel. Southworth admitted to writing the novel while her son was ill and her sister was dying: "It was the saddest time in my life" (qtd. in Dobson,

"Introduction" xxvi). She found in Capitola's adventures a relief from her anxieties. It is possible that she was better able to censor herself in her other sentimental writing than she was at this particularly stressful time in her life.[9]

In its attention to regional difference, the environmental determinants of Capitola's character, and the marketplace, *The Hidden Hand* anticipated literary realism. In this last respect, it may also have built upon innovations pioneered by slave narratives and antislavery newspapers. Augusta Rohrbach links the origins of literary realism to the antislavery campaign, arguing that both share a preoccupation with money and the marketplace. The antislavery campaign successfully commercialized a humanitarian movement, making marketplace transactions carry political import. On the one hand, the antislavery campaign encouraged consumers to boycott slave products such as sugar and cotton; on the other hand, it encouraged right-minded consumers to purchase antislavery gift books, medallions, samplers, and slave narratives. Advertisements in William Lloyd Garrison's *Liberator* urged consumers to frequent vendors who were politically like-minded. Antislavery literature differed from other reform literature in its emphasis on product tie-ins such as free labor sugar. Antislavery literature showed a preoccupation with the connection between "morality and money" (xiv), Rohrbach argues.

It is fitting, then, that *The Hidden Hand* is ultimately adapted for the stage[10] and spawns a variety of consumer spin-offs, including Capitola hats and suits for female consumers hoping to emulate their tomboy heroine (Hudock 10).[11] Capitola comes full circle. The heroine is sensitized to the specific material oppression of women through her early exposure to gendered employment conditions in the North. She can only survive in the New York streets as a boy given the limited options available to working-class girls. And like Capitola, her female fans saw the marketplace as a means by which to adopt the look and hopefully the privileges of the tomboy.

Coming 15 years after Lydia Maria Child's depictions of urban life and in an era of escalating regional tensions, Southworth permitted herself none of the ambivalence Child showed toward the wage labor system. The novel fully endorses wage labor, individualism, and class mobility as Southworth imagines their importation into the South. Serialized in the *Ledger*, the novel, like the literary periodical, reveled in the possibilities opened up by urban life. Articles published alongside Southworth's novel similarly extolled city life. One article upbraids New York newspapers for "never neglect[ing] an opportunity for exhibiting the worst of city life, and of exaggerating the perils and dangers of living in our streets" ("Not near So Bad as We Seem"). Another marvels at the city's "diversity": "But what is more wonderful still, [*sic*] is the human composition of New York. By the census of 1851, nearly one-half of the population was born in Europe!... What diversity!" ("Our City"). While the paper is late to comment upon the Civil War—no mention is ever made of the firing on Fort Sumter or to sectional tensions until three months after the outbreak of war—it is quite vocal on the issue of women's rights, defending the ability of women to write book reviews and publishing a weekly column by Fanny Fern commonly devoted to attacking negative stereotypes of women. In other words, the paper comports with *The Hidden Hand* in its yoking together of two liberal agendas—capitalist individualism and women's rights.

The remarkable achievement of *The Hidden Hand* is that it captured a popular audience while defying generic conventions. Southworth's antislavery commitments did not result in a more complex characterization of African Americans or even in any serious condemnation of slavery per se. But these antislavery commitments did enable her to challenge hegemonic characterizations of women and cities. She did not so much appropriate antislavery narratives and icons as turn them on their heads, eliminating the supplicating slave and revealing the martyred white woman to be largely ineffective. In their place are comic figures. Wool challenges Major Wargrave but with plausible deniability. Capitola eschews martyrdom and confrontation in favor of parody and spectacle. Moreover, the novel, in its anticipation of realism, encouraged both readers and theater goers to examine women's roles in the marketplace and to imagine the marketplace as an empowering place for women. The language and iconography of antislavery animated this vision of a marketplace in which white women could and should shed their purportedly natural roles in an organic culture to possess and market new versions of self.

"THE WHITE SLAVE OF THE NORTH": LOWELL MILL WOMEN AND THE EVOLUTION OF "FREE LABOR"

In her first attempt to represent female factory workers to a critical public, Harriet Farley, future editor of the *Lowell Offering*, attacked Orestes Brownson for his "slander" of working-class women. Brownson, a transcendentalist reformer and 1840 presidential candidate, had published an article warning of the emergence of a debased and exploited working class in America. "The Laboring Classes" was part of a series of controversial articles articulating his electoral platform, and it was to become a well-known analysis of early American industrialism. In the article, Brownson equated independence with an individual's ownership of the means of production, a cornerstone of American republicanism in the early nineteenth century. He contested the more recent characterization of wage laborers as "free" workers en route to becoming self-employed farmers, craftsmen, or professionals. Challenging this assumption of economic mobility for workers, he asked, "[I]s there a reasonable chance that any considerable portion of the present generation of laborers, shall ever become owners of a sufficient portion of the funds of production, to be able to sustain themselves by laboring on their own capital, that is, as independent laborers? . . . everybody knows there is not" (371). Without this form of independence, Brownson went on to argue, American workers faced a degradation worse than African American slavery.

Harriet Farley might have been expected to agree with Brownson. By 1840, she had worked in the Lowell, Massachusetts, mills for eight years, during which time the owners had reduced wages, imposed work speedups, increased rents at the company-owned boarding houses where most of the female operatives lived, and defeated two strikes by the women. Farley's rebuttal to Brownson—and many of her future editorials in the *Lowell Offering*—expressed concern over deteriorating pay and work conditions for women at the mills. At the same time, Farley and most of the other writers for the *Lowell Offering* resisted representations of the mills that conflated the mill's harsh environment with the degradation of women workers. To defend women's decisions to work in the mills, Farley developed an alternative to Brownson's masculinist definition of independence, one informed by her experience as both a mill operative and the daughter of a farmer. She repeatedly claimed that wage labor in the mills offered greater independence than women's lives on family-owned farms.

Taking a page from the antislavery feminists, the first sustained women's movement in the country, mill women used the tropes of the antislavery campaign to refigure their earlier rural lives as lives of dependence and domestic servitude not unlike slavery. If wage labor in the mills was restrictive and exploitative, so too was farm labor at home for women. Independence based on capital ownership was elusive, at best, for women. By building on the campaign of the antislavery feminists, writers for the *Lowell Offering* formed an alternative to Orestes Brownson's masculinist discourse of class. Independence for these women became something vastly different than Brownson imagined—the freedom to change their domestic situations, leave oppressive homes, reunite fractured families, move geographically, and, above all, participate in a marketplace that conferred social esteem.

Brownson's article suggested that factory women participated in not one but two marketplaces, and when they bartered their labor they also bartered their marriageability; she who sought to profit in the labor market might lose all in the marriage market.

> Few of them ever marry; fewer still ever return to their native places with reputations unimpaired. "She has worked in a Factory," is almost enough to damn to infamy the most worthy and virtuous girl. (370)

Leaving her family to live in the factory-owned boarding houses in Lowell, a woman also left the protection of her family, and, according to

Brownson, she was widely believed to fall prey to predatory city men. Similar depictions of the British working class, the premiere nineteenth-century example of a degraded and exploited people, populated the penny press and reformist tracts. It was this picture of promiscuous female workers, a picture Farley believed to be imported from entirely different conditions in Britain, that the *Lowell Offering* was devoted to stamping out.[1]

When Farley responded to Brownson in the pages of the *Lowell Offering*, she left unanswered Brownson's claim that factory wages were insufficient for male or female operatives to establish themselves on independent farms or businesses. Nor did she comment on the health and working conditions of operatives. Instead, in an essay that would set the tone for her later editorship of the *Lowell Offering*, Farley offered a definition of independence at odds with Brownson's:

> And whom has Mr. Brownson slandered? . . . girls who generally come from quiet country homes where their minds and manners have been formed under the eyes of the worthy sons of Pilgrims and their virtuous partners and who return again to become the wives of the free intelligent yeomenry of New England and the mothers of quite a proportion of our future republicans.
>
> (A Factory Girl 17)

Farley defended female operatives by removing them from their factory context and by downplaying their independence from family ties. Positioning them back in their rural homes, "under the eyes" of their fathers, husbands, and sons, Farley secured their reputations by denying their autonomy in the Lowell mills. Farley insisted, however, that female factory operatives achieved independence vicariously, through the men in their families. She further argued that they chose to exercise their independence by "voluntarily assuming" certain "restraints" (17).

> [I]t has been asserted that to put ourselves under the influence and restraints of corporate bodies is contrary to the spirit of our institutions and to the love of independence we ought to cherish. There is a spirit of independence which is averse to social life itself and I would advise all those who wish to cherish it to go far beyond the Rocky Mountains and hold communion with none but the untamed Indian and the wild beast of the forest. (17)

If Brownson used a racialized metaphor to characterize white, working-class women as degraded, Farley responded in kind. Both the black slave and the "untamed Indian" represented easily identifiable extremes on the outside of American republicanism. The truly "independent" white woman, using Brownson's definition, would have to own her own productive property. She could not marry, since, under antebellum law, she would then cede ownership of her property and person to her husband. Even unmarried women were unlikely to be economically self-sufficient unless they came from wealthy families. To the lower-middle-class women attracted to the Lowell mills, such independent women would have existed outside of their social milieu. Like the "untamed" Indian, Brownson's "independent" woman seemed outside "social life itself."

While Brownson hoped to recruit working-class supporters, including women, his use of seduction metaphors and slave metaphors to characterize their shift to wage labor alienated them. Brownson assumed that the factory operatives sacrificed freedoms to accept the fetters of factory life, that women had been forced off farms as their families fell into the proletariat or lured away from more independent rural work. Yet the writers in the *Lowell Offering* very carefully measured the freedoms and limitations inherent in rural and urban life, concluding that as producers, consumers, and potential wives and mothers, their options were enhanced by factory work. Brownson's appeal was couched in terms that did not appeal to rural women, who seldom independently owned the farms they cultivated and who understood their life options to be largely determined by their family context. His assumptions regarding working-class self-identity have been repeated by labor historians who have persistently evaluated the motivations of working-class people in masculinist terms.[2] The rhetoric working-class organizers used to mobilize workers frequently contained gendered language and imagery that appealed less to women than men. Labor historian Ava Baron questions the analytical framework that labor organizers and labor historians have traditionally used to represent women's working-class identity. She suggests, "Rather than ask why women have been difficult to organize, ask 'What assumptions about gender have been structured into unions?'" Rather than ask why women workers resisted Brownson's movement, this chapter asks two fundamental questions. How did the gendered and racialized tropes of the antislavery campaign shape women's response to factory work? How did factory work and American attitudes toward such work impact women's sense of their sexuality?

The stories, essays, and sketches of the *Lowell Offering* would use metaphors of slavery and seduction, but not as Brownson had. As David Roediger writes, "As long as slavery thrived, any attempt to come to grips with wage labor tended to lapse into exaggerated metaphors or frantic denials of those metaphors" (*The Wages of Whiteness* 87). Writers for the *Lowell Offering* resisted either a simple conflation of slave and factory laborer or a too frantic denial of crucial similarities. The women writers would promote an understanding of wage labor as a positive alternative to both the antisocial independence Brownson represented and the slavish dependence rural life and family life could entail.

Because tales of women's economic exploitation were quickly transformed into images of sexual exploitation in the public mind, the writers for the *Lowell Offering* resisted dramatizations of the mills' most abusive practices. Never in the paper's five-year run (1840–45) is any reference made to the two failed strikes of 1834 and 1836, though in both cases the mill owners retaliated against labor leaders. And the editors, particularly Harriet Farley, vehemently denied that the long hours, hot and humid conditions, dirty air, or rushed meals impaired the health of workers. However, following the example of the antislavery feminists, the writers often evaluated their independence and empowerment by carefully analyzing their domestic economy.

The antislavery feminists seldom commented on the exploitative nature of slavery's work relationship; however, they were far more likely than their male counterparts to criticize slavery's impact on family relations. Some male antislavery activists—Orestes Brownson among them before he renounced antislavery—argued that the slave and the wage laborer shared a common exploitation: both worked on the productive capital of another who had far more power over the terms of employment than they did. The former slave Frederick Douglass described the use of slave, free black, and white wage laborers at Baltimore shipyards as part of a continuum in his 1854 autobiography, *My Bondage and My Freedom*. But these arguments were eclipsed by the family protection campaign that dominated the antislavery press after Angelina and Sarah Grimke's speaking tour in 1837–8.

When the working-class women writing for the *Lowell Offering* articulated their own agenda as women and workers, they found in the antislavery family protection campaign a way to critique their traditional roles without undermining their already maligned public image. Rather than fight the deterioration of wages and work conditions in the Lowell mills by insisting on their victimization and enslavement, a strategy labor leaders from Orestes Brownson to George Henry Evans employed on their behalf, Farley insisted on workers' rights as "the daughters of freemen" and as "Yankee daughters" who would not work in the mills if conditions deteriorated further.[3] Along with all of the writers for the *Lowell Offering*, she rejected the label "white slave of the North," a term used to arouse reformers on behalf of women workers. She preferred to become a social leader rather than an object of social reform.[4]

FUGITIVE FARMERS AND FREE FACTORY OPERATIVES

The *Lowell Offering* began in 1840 as a collection of stories, poems, and essays written by women mill workers in their self-improvement circle. To demonstrate "what factory girls had power to do," the women, together with Lowell's Universalist minister, Reverend Abel C. Thomas, issued the monthly 30-page serial. It was the first serial written and published by American factory women, and it met with an overwhelmingly positive response. Not only did mill workers and their families purchase subscriptions, but Americans and even Europeans interested in the intellectual endeavors of factory workers supported the serial. Initially sponsored by Reverend Thomas, the paper was purchased by long-term factory workers and editors Harriet Farley and Harriott Curtis in 1843. The paper's success in America and in Europe was due in part to its reputation as a grassroots publication, but the positive attention it drew to the Lowell mills as a singularly enlightened industrial experiment made it an attractive public relations tool to the mill owners. When the paper was threatened with declining subscriptions in 1844 and 1845, mill owners bought back subscriptions and supplemented the pay of the editors. The mill owners' support undermined the paper's reputation among mill women, and the paper folded in 1845. At its peak, however, it was a cause célèbre among New Englanders.

Antislavery reformers, in particular, patronized the paper. When Harriet Farley published a select list of the *Lowell Offering*'s "friends" in 1843, it read like a who's who among abolitionists—William Ellery Channing, John Greenleaf Whittier, Eliza Follen, Maria Weston Chapman, Elizabeth Peabody, Emma Willard, and British antislavery reformer Harriet Martineau all praised the paper. Interestingly, none of the reformers who were listed as patrons of the *Lowell Offering* were much involved in labor reforms. Other antislavery activists were more outspoken champions of the working class, including William Lloyd Garrison, Frederick Douglass, and Gerritt Smith.[5] Despite attempts by antislavery reformers like these to forge a political coalition between wage laborers and slaves by stressing their common exploitation, the writers for the *Lowell Offering* found little rhetorical power in the comparisons others drew between them and denied similarities between their condition as wage workers and that of female slaves. A careful examination of the *Lowell Offering* reveals that their appropriation of antislavery tropes facilitated an acceptance of the wage relationship. The mill women's use of tropes from slave narratives demonstrates their familiarity with the antislavery family protection campaign and its applicability to the specific situation of first-generation working-class women.[6] The anti-patriarchal implications of the family protection campaign influenced their view of marriage and farm life.

The lead article of the *Lowell Offering*'s first issue builds on the genre of the slave narrative and the figure of the tragic mulatta. At a time when the American seduction story, in which a woman is ruined by her susceptibility to a predatory man, had gone into eclipse everywhere except in antislavery literature, "History of a Hemlock Broom: Written by Itself," tells the story of a woman seduced into domestic servitude.[7] Using an extended metaphor, the author cautiously approaches the very sensitive topics of women's sexual and economic oppression. The hemlock branch envies those who travel, wanting "a sight of things hidden" from her (Hannah 1). In highly gendered terms, the hemlock branch describes her predicament: "The thought that I must ever remain fixed to my parent tree, while many objects around me were possessed of the power of locomotion, was a great grief to me..." (1). She is severed from the "parent tree" by a "farm-yard acquaintance," who, with "his eyes fixed earnestly upon me [...], brandished a large jack knife" and completed "the work of separation" (1). She comments, "Now then was my wish accomplished. I felt that I was free and grateful to my deliverer" (1). However, she is quickly disillusioned when she is dragged across the field, broken up, and attached to an old handle. "I was not his first companion and feared I should not be his last" (1). She becomes "more thin and bare" and with "severe self-reproach" asks her friend Hannah to transcribe her story and circulate it in Lowell, commenting that the story "simple as it is; has yet a moral" (2).

Clearly, a parallel might be drawn between the bare and wasted hemlock broom and the overworked factory operative. The longing to break away from parents and see faraway places motivated many of the women who were approached by male recruiters in their rural communities. The 70-hour weeks, which were routine for Lowell workers, broke the health of some women. Many of the stories in the *Lowell Offering* also romanticize rural life as a pastoral paradise. In this reading, the story acts as a warning to prospective factory operatives who might undervalue their rural origins.

But ultimately, the hemlock broom entrusts her story to Hannah, who is not dissuaded from her plan to work in the mills by the story's "moral." In fact, the broom hopes she will go to Lowell where the story can be told more widely. Moreover, the broom laments her new, specifically domestic, situation.[8] She is no longer attached to the "parent tree," but yoked to an old broom handle inside of the house. Starting as the best broom and used in the parlor, eventually, she is fit only for cleaning the kitchen grate. The stories in the *Lowell Offering* repeatedly describe the lures of a romantic union turning into the drudgery of domestic servitude; writers contrast the harried farm wife to her good-humored, useful counterpart, the "old maid." Describing the broom's "deliverer" as a "farm-yard acquaintance" whose eyes were "fixed earnestly upon her" suggests she is betrayed by her lover and ruined by her domestic responsibilities rather than by work outside the home.

One might argue for either interpretation, but what is most important is the ambivalence this story captures. The female factory operatives of Lowell had limited options. The overwhelming majority of these women came from small New England farms and knew the exhausting work that fell to the wives of farmers. They knew as farm wives they would have little control over the farm's profits and little disposable income. Letters home frequently cited the ability to earn an independent income, one not shared with family members, as the primary motivation for working in the Lowell factories (Dublin, *Farm to Factory* 23). While the pieties of true womanhood mediated against open expressions of discontent with domestic life on the farm, particularly for working-class women who were already sensitive to popular prejudice against themselves, women could criticize domestic restrictions through displacement. Analogies between women's work and slavery cut in unexpected ways for first-generation working-class women. Specifically, they may have seen the South's peculiar "domestic institution" as one more closely approximating their mothers' lives as farm wives than their own as factory operatives.

The shared experience of domestic restrictions suggests why writers for the *Lowell Offering* turned to antislavery rhetoric to describe their former rural lives. As the hemlock branch served as a vehicle for expressing anxiety over the options for working-class women, so too did the figure of the tragic mulatta become a means of discussing sexual violence and oppression in slavery and, more generally, in marriage. At a time when women asserted their power by claiming to transcend sexuality and desire, domestic writers found it difficult to discuss men's power over their persons as well as their property in marriage. One way around the tabooed subject of sexual slavery in marriage was to displace the narrative of sexual violence onto the tragic mulatta who was reduced to a possession. These stories often explicitly drew the connection between the tragic mulatta's fate and that of her free, white counterpart in marriage. In both the antislavery stories and in this, the lead article of the very first *Lowell Offering*, we see the beginnings of the seduction story's reemergence as a tale of gendered class oppression.

In addition, the story's title, "History of a Hemlock Broom: Written By Itself," makes a more direct appropriation of antislavery discourse. As in slave narratives, which were conventionally subtitled "written by himself" or "written by herself," the hemlock broom tells her own story, calling attention to the self-conscious subjectivity of the "author." When history is told by the slave, when the worker becomes the subject and object of history, the slave and the worker reassert the connection between their personhood and the mode of production. They cease to be objects of reform to be patronized and become participants in the process of social revisioning and change. Factory women wanted this voice.

In another adaptation of antislavery narratives, girls and women escape domestic abuse by running away to the factory. Like fugitive slaves, these domestic fugitives flee demeaning work conditions and humiliation. For example, in "Tales of Factory Life, No. 1," Sarah T. runs away from the abusive Mrs. J. for whom she works as a live-in servant paid only room and board. Mrs. J. rails against the factories, fearing they will "take [Sarah] off" and warns Sarah that she will be stigmatized by working in the factory. Still, the barefooted Sarah runs away to Lowell hoping to save for an education. En route, she meets kind, like-minded travelers who help her to escape. Lowell, like the North in slave narratives, becomes the counterpoint to the oppressive circumstances from which the author escapes.

In another story, ironically titled "Woman's Influence," Clara Huntley flees her intemperate, surly husband, Ernest. The narrator warns single women that marriage is a loss of power and identity, that the one man a woman cannot influence is her husband:

> All mankind are perverse, and love power; and all husbands, especially, love to show that they are masters at home, although their own errors are masters of their own hearts. And when we teach that it is a woman's influence that is to restrain and reform the errors of society, it ought always to be added, that a wife may not reprove a husband's transgressions, neither by showing that she is grieved, nor by unkind, harsh, or measured words. By marriage a woman loses her identity, and the husband but regards her as his "better half." Hence, her admonitions are like those of his own conscience, unwelcome visitors, which he will fly from if he can.
>
> (Grace 220)

A woman's loss of identity in marriage makes her husband her "master," and his love of power makes him set his will against her. Marriage becomes a sado-masochistic partnership; by becoming an extension of her husband's power, his "better half," the wife enhances her own power as well, since her identity now derives from his. Single women, the narrator infers, willingly exchange their independence for this unreliable form of power. But when the master becomes a slave to his own "errors," his wife loses even more power and status than he, and her "influence" is useless against his passions.

The antislavery feminists began their analysis of slavery at exactly this point. They countered the popular impression that slavery as a system was beneficial because most masters were benevolent. They, too, were skeptical of the power of "woman's influence." In antislavery literature, most masters, even benevolent ones, were subject to destructive passions that could not be countered by moral suasion or feminine influence. Without the power to physically leave their "masters" and sustain themselves, both slaves and women were left with only one effective alternative: they could influence their "masters" through self-sacrifice, the ultimate extreme of which was self-destruction. In Harriet Beecher Stowe's antislavery classic, *Uncle Tom's Cabin*, Mr. Shelby covers his losses from speculation by selling two slaves. He knows his wife will rebuke him, but never considers consulting her. Her willingness to sell her jewelry to save Uncle Tom and little Harry fails to dissuade him. As several incidents in the novel indicate, only a slave's or woman's death enables them to influence their owners. Eva persuades her father to free his slaves on her deathbed. Uncle Tom's death fires George Shelby's determination to fight slavery as a system and is meant to similarly fire the reader's opposition to slavery. Women and slaves do effectively oppose their "masters," however, by stealing themselves. George and Eliza, Cassy and Emmeline run away from their owners. Similarly, when Clara Huntley of "Woman's Influence" chooses to run away to Lowell, she rejects death as a means of influencing Ernest. Instead, she deprives her husband of his possession of her to provoke his renunciation of alcohol. She chooses independence over influence.

For Lowell women, factory work represented enhanced freedom and independence; yet, this new found state presented problems as well as possibilities. When Clara chooses to leave Ernest, to break the bonds of dependence that had previously defined her life, she becomes despondent. The story concludes with a reformed Ernest rediscovering Clara, nearly broken by her years of isolation. In this story, influence without the real threat of leaving Ernest is impotent. But Clara's direct attack on male prerogative and her strike for independence, in and of themselves, provide no happiness or satisfaction. Only when they result in a more powerful influence over Ernest, only when he returns a reformed man, is she permitted a happy ending. It remains an open question how female readers would have read the ideological import of this story. If they emphasized the ending, they may have felt the model of female influence to have been vindicated. What matters in this story for such readers would have been Ernest's conversion. But if the vision of Clara taking charge of her own life prevailed, readers may have embraced a model of economic independence and identified with the self-respecting Clara who will not allow Ernest to humiliate her. For these readers,

Ernest's return would have been a footnote to a story about a woman choosing self-respect and independence over a misguided notion of wifely duty.

In the majority of the stories in the *Lowell Offering,* women prove their independence by going to Lowell and then choosing to return to the restraints of their homes, renouncing the lures of the marketplace in favor of the nonmarket value of the homestead. One story in the magazine details the transition from a young girl's dangerous independence to her willing subjugation to her family, described in terms of her greater self-possession. In "Abby's Year in Lowell," a headstrong, adolescent girl leaves her family for openly self-interested reasons, to buy a new dress. But she revises her aims when she discovers that she is to be "abandoned to herself" (Lucinda 4). The narrator commends her "self-distrust" and details her journey from self-centeredness through self-denial to self-possession, which entitles her to return within the family fold as a treasured member. Most remarkably, once Abby is in Lowell, she resists the dress shops more easily than the confectioneries.

> It was hard to walk by the milliner's shops with an unwavering step; and when she came to the confectioneries, she could not help stopping... When she saw fine strawberries, she said to herself, "I can gather them in our own pasture next year;" when she looked upon the nice peaches, cherries, and plums, which stood in tempting array behind their crystal barriers, she said again, "I will do without them this summer;" and when apples, pears, and nuts were offered to her for sale, she thought that she would eat none of them till she went home. (5)

She is most tempted by that which had never before been a commodity but had been easily available on her family farm. Abby's encounter with the marketplace makes her nostalgic for the nonmarket values of the farm where the fruits and nuts are not only free, they are symbolic of all that lay outside the market and all that she did not properly value before leaving home.

In establishing her new, "independent" identity, what Abby actually discovers is the "interdependence" central to her character. While the pleasures of the marketplace attracted many Lowell mill women, such pleasures did involve an anxiety-provoking separation from the restrictive structures of rural family life. Questions of self-possession became particularly fraught for women who gained esteem from being other-centered. As Gillian Brown has argued, women in the nineteenth century attempted to establish models of individualism that functioned on different principles than those for men.

> Against the self-interest of the typically male individualism Tocqueville analyzed, the subculture women image is based on self-denial and collectivity—the ethos of sympathy customarily and disparagingly called sentimentalism. In this view, women thus claim and typify an anti-market (if not anti-masculine) individualism... the alignment between individualism and domesticity might structure dispositions other than self-interest, such as self-denial and self-protection. (6)

In Abby's nostalgia for fruit from her family's farm, she shows a new found appreciation for that which lies outside the market exchange. Her act of self-denial, manifested in her rejection of the marketplace's pleasures, becomes, ironically, a step toward greater individuation and self-possession. "Abandoned to herself," she proves herself worthy of her family's esteem. She gains self-possession, the goal of both the antislavery movement and the early women's movement, to the extent that she resists the selfish pleasures of the marketplace and identifies herself with others. True independence, for Abby, comes from denying herself pleasures in the city in order to purchase treats for her family whose happiness and surprise at her self-control she can enjoy. Abby's year in Lowell enables her to return to the family in a different position. Because she has had the opportunity to engage in selfish pleasures and has successfully resisted them, her contributions to the family take on a greater significance. They are the result of choice rather than duty and consequently earn her greater respect.

However, as much as a story of family devotion may have advanced the *Lowell Offering*'s professed goal of improving the status of factory women, it did not accurately reflect the motivations of Lowell women. Thomas Dublin's study of New England's female textile workers between 1830 and 1860 suggests women had more self-interested motives for migrating to Lowell. According to his survey of their letters, most of the women planned to buy clothes they could not otherwise afford, save for their own educations, or save for a dowry (*From Farm to Factory* 19–23). Dublin concludes that American women of the period, unlike their European counterparts, were not expected to contribute to the family economy. While "work outside the home in nineteenth-century Europe was basically an adaptation of the traditional family economy within a changed economic setting," the same type of employment for American women represented a distinct break with previous patterns of female work (23–24).

The reluctance of the *Lowell Offering*'s writers to publicize their financial independence suggests their ambivalence toward their emerging status as "free" wage laborers. Freedom and independence had their negative, antisocial connotations, as Farley's comparison between the "spirit of independence" and the "untamed Indian" suggested. If, at one extreme, Brownson viewed female factory operatives as slaves to the mill owners, Farley suggested that Brownson placed himself outside society altogether. He rejected not only "slavish" dependence, in which one person dominates over another, but a more egalitarian interdependence in his masculinized social vision. Women ultimately made a distinction between independence, with its antisocial connotation, and freedom. Women's freedom consisted of choosing which restraints they would subject themselves to. When Abby chooses not to buy the dresses of which she has dreamed, but to buy gifts for her siblings and save for her future family, she has exercised a freedom Brownson had not contemplated, a form of self-possession derived from self-denial.

THE CHASTE MILL GIRL: FROM FREE FACTORY OPERATIVE TO MACHINE SLAVE

As discussed earlier, many historians have debated the relationship between industrial capitalism and the rise of an organized antislavery movement in the nineteenth century. Antebellum apologists for slavery, and even some who opposed slavery, accused capitalists of using the issue of slavery to deflect attention away from the degradation of workers closer to home. In Britain, it was the elite African Institution and wealthy philanthropists, without a base among the majority of British citizens, who initially pushed laws against the slave trade through parliament. Only after their legislative success did a mass antislavery movement develop in Britain and the United States. The capitalists who comprised the African Institution, whether conscious of it or not, advanced a definition of "free labor" that legitimated the exploitation of British wage laborers, who, in contrast to slaves, "freely" entered work contracts. They had the choice to reject individual work contracts, though in practice this choice could be illusory. All available work might offer subsistence wages and dangerous work conditions. Nonetheless, compared with slaves, the wage laborer could be defined as "free."

Orestes Brownson renounced his own antislavery activism because he believed that the antislavery movement was being used to displace more important concerns about the growth of a wage-dependent laboring class in America. However, in the United States, antislavery activism developed much differently. Considering the development of a powerful antislavery base among the working class and among the growing professional-managerial class in America, historian John Ashworth argues that antislavery discourses had surprising implications for Americans of all classes. As more and more workers ceased to own the means of production or control the mode of production, other people increasingly controlled their daily activities and their standards of living. To dampen the incentive that individuals had to exploit others, Americans of all classes sought institutions that would limit the areas in which self-interest governed human relations. "They looked for, and found, new supports for individual morality and the social order. Among these were the family, the home, and the individual conscience" (Ashworth, *American Historical Review* 822). In a culture that increasingly viewed family affections as a bulwark against antisocial behavior, slavery and its subordination of family relations to market relations would appear to all classes to be profoundly destabilizing. In other words, the institution of slavery was increasingly understood to be more than a system for organizing the Southern economy; it also organized—and distorted—the family and individual conscience.

To Brownson, the writers for the *Lowell Offering* rebuffed a friend when they denounced his article. He assumed that laboring on a family farm was a form of independence for women, an independence they were duped into rejecting when they left for the factories. His patriarchal view of rural domestic economies colored his view of female operatives' decisions. These first-generation working-class women, positioned as they were between the family farm and the factory, hastened the acceptance of the new definition of "free" labor. Using comparisons to the fugitive slave, writers for the *Lowell Offering* characterized factory labor as a means of escaping oppressive domestic situations and enhancing their choices in the kinds of families they would freely establish. Factory labor also became a means of repairing and reestablishing the family on a more stable financial footing. Through the family protection campaign of the feminist-abolitionists, the writers for the *Lowell Offering* learned to prize their freedom as the freedom to leave and to return to better homes rather than to independently own their homes. Freedom meant having the ability to participate in the marketplace but also having the self-possession necessary to refuse the marketplace's lure if it conflicted with their families' interests.

This freedom to choose between farm and factory was not, however, full independence. In Farley's formulation, women's independence originated in that of their fathers, husbands, and sons. When mill owners cut wages, Farley's definition of independence encouraged them to return home "by choice" rather than stay and fight for higher wages. Unfortunately, the derivative nature of Farley's definition impeded the effective organizing of mill workers as New England-born farmers' daughters were replaced with immigrant labor that could not choose to leave the factory in the face of declining wages and work speedups. After 1836, there were no more strikes at Lowell; native-born women left the mills as mill work became less remunerative.

The writers for the *Lowell Offering* applied the antislavery family protection campaign to their experience in ways male labor leaders like Orestes Brownson could not have anticipated. The factory offered an outlet from oppressive or disempowering domestic situations. Some fled to the factory as fugitive slaves fled North. Others came with greater circumspection, but their ability to leave the factory at will—and most did leave after only a few years—made it difficult to accept Orestes Brownson's comparisons between themselves and slaves. As an organizing tool among these women workers, comparisons to slavery did not capture their experience of the factories. Instead, antislavery tropes better represented their experience of farm labor and facilitated the acceptance of wage labor.

As Lowell women distanced themselves from the rhetoric and often the working-class organizations of reformers like Orestes Brownson, they began to develop their own critique of market culture and machine culture. A comparison between the *Lowell Offering* and male-dominated working-class papers will show that the writers walked a fine line between the patronizing representations of women workers in working-class papers and the degrading representations of factory women in middle-class publications. The *Lowell Offering*'s writers considered comparisons between their condition and the slaves' insulting and inaccurate, but they were, nevertheless, concerned with economic changes that threatened their relationship to work and family in ways they could express through antislavery iconography. They were on the forefront of economic changes in which human labor was increasingly adapted to the pace and rhythms of the machine and in which more types of work were compensated formally through a sometimes arbitrary marketplace.[9] Their stories considered the ramifications of an increasingly rationalized economy, while working-class, male-dominated papers focused more narrowly on the material conditions of wage workers and small property owners. The more comprehensive view of mill women was a result, in part, of their receptiveness to the antislavery critique of the marketplace.

In my introduction, I argue that the antislavery feminists invented no new arguments against slavery. As early as Samuel Sewall's 1700 pamphlet, "The Selling of Joseph," Americans denounced slavery's disregard for family relations. The antislavery feminists, however, popularized this argument with lurid stories of anguished mothers torn from their children and slave women sold for concubines. This argument resonated more powerfully in the North as an increasingly ubiquitous marketplace threatened the economic stability and integrity of families. Women, in particular, faced dramatic changes in their relationship to their families.

The families whose daughters worked in the mills lived on the border between the old, rural middle class and either the wage-dependent working class or the new middle class. The Lowell mill women were in a key position to help their families navigate this transition as many of them used their wages to establish younger children in the emerging middle-class professions. Domestic ideology was propagated primarily by women from this socioeconomic sphere. They limited the size of their families, placed a heavier emphasis on children's education and character development, and encouraged their sons to delay entrance into the work force and to deny themselves market pleasures in order to train for the new middle-class professions (Coontz 184–90). The antislavery movement's family protection campaign was the most radical expression of the new domestic ideology. Its picture of families threatened by a hostile commercial and political sphere was central to the new domestic ideology, but unlike the conservative branch of this rhetoric, it specifically called upon women to reshape the commercial and political spheres to better harmonize with the domestic ethos. Mill women strongly supported the antislavery movement. Lucy Larcom remarked in her autobiography, "If the vote of the millgirls had been taken, it would doubtless have been unanimous on the antislavery side" (qtd. in Alvez 142). Harriet Farley invited the famous abolitionist poet John Greenleaf Whittier to address the factory operatives' self-improvement circle (Alvez 143). Antislavery petitions were very successful among factory operatives, and the *Lowell Offering* never printed the disparaging comments about organized antislavery that characterized many other working-class papers. The female operatives supported abolitionists because they recognized in antislavery discourse manifestations of their worst fears—broken families, degrading work conditions, sexual exploitation, and a fixed caste system.

Writers for the *Lowell Offering* went beyond a focus on compensation and economic security, a focus typical of other working-class papers, to develop a critique of both market and machine culture that anticipated the development of the realist novel. They were more likely than their male counterparts to speculate about the underlying cultural implications of an economy run more and more exclusively on the basis of exchange values.

I have chosen the *Working Man's Advocate* and the *Voice of Industry* as representative male-dominated working-class papers because they were relatively successful and were published by clearly identified working-class reform organizations, the *Working Man's Advocate* by the National Reform Association in New York and the *Voice of Industry* by the New England Workingmen's Association in Massachusetts. Looking at issues of these two papers during the last two years of the *Lowell Offering*'s publication, in 1844 and 1845, it becomes clear how unusual the *Lowell Offering*'s use of antislavery tropes and narratives was.

The *Working Man's Advocate* was first published in 1829 under the auspices of the Working Men's Movement in New York City. The paper folded in 1835 and its editor, George Henry Evans, retreated to the countryside while unionization efforts in New York City foundered. When Evans resumed its publication in 1844, the paper reflected a shift in Evans's thinking away from unionization and toward agrarian reform. The paper became an integral part of the National Reform Association's (NRA) appeal to disaffected artisans, encouraging these "white slaves" to "Vote Yourself a Farm." The NRA proposed developing egalitarian (and white) townships in the West composed of equal 160-acre farms.[10]

The *Voice of Industry* was a more comprehensive paper than the *Working Man's Advocate*, investigating a wider range of reforms and devoting many of its pages to the specific experiences of women in a range of occupations. The *Voice of Industry* provides an especially useful comparison to the *Lowell Offering* because it included among its founding editors Sarah Bagley, a former writer for the *Lowell Offering*. Bagley, in fact, explicitly attacked the *Lowell Offering* for its refusal to include some of her articles critical of the corporation. The *Voice of Industry* was eventually published from Lowell, Massachusetts, as a mobilizing tool for the New England Workingmen's Association, an organization more devoted to unionization than the NRA, but sufficiently similar to establish formal connections to the NRA in 1845.[11] Unlike the *Working Man's Advocate*, the *Voice of Industry* explicitly represented working women, though, as will be seen, they were envisioned as an auxiliary, largely decorative segment of the New England Workingmen's Association.

In Evans's opening editorial advertising the newly reestablished *Working Man's Advocate*, he described the "present condition" of the "laboring classes" by comparing Northern and Southern systems of exploitation:

> Let us look around. At the *South*, the master lives in opulence on the labor of his *colored* slaves, whose stimulus to exertion is too often the driver's lash, but who are, almost universally, provided with the absolute necessaries of life in all stages of their existence. At the *North*, the master has a lash more potent than the whipthong to stimulate the energies of his *white* slaves; *the fear of want*.
>
> ("To the Public")

Like many proslavery apologists, Evans argued that the Northern worker was no more independent than the slave, though quite a bit less secure, even less materially comfortable. Consequently, Evans considered "white slavery" a more unjust system and a higher priority for reformers. In a subsequent article, Evans starkly depicts abolition as a distraction from the more important struggle for white, working-class rights:

> We are opposed to *every form of slavery*, but if we were compelled, under the present system of land monopoly, to choose between the northern factory or the southern plantation, *we would jump at the latter* . . . Should the black desire to transfer himself from the one form of slavery to the other, we would not throw a straw in his way; but we would not *persuade* him into the suicidal act. In our opinion, until the negro can get his *land* as well as his body, he is better off as he is.
>
> ("The People's Cause.")

Evans clearly encouraged his readers to view working class struggle as a white cause and as a cause undermined by abolitionist efforts. While he would not discourage an individual slave from running away, Evans did actively discourage organized abolitionist efforts by attacking abolitionist leaders and by seeking to undermine British working-class support for abolition.

In a public letter to Gerrit Smith, one of the wealthy reformers who funded abolitionist projects, Evans called him "one of the largest Slaveholders in the United States" ("To Gerrit Smith"). Smith owned much land in upstate New York, land that Smith would one day use to develop a settlement for freed slaves. For Evans, having more land than Smith's family could cultivate made Smith a "slaveholder" who lived upon the labor of others. Using one of the abolitionists' own evangelical techniques, he asked Smith, "[. . .W]hat shall you do to be saved?" ("To Gerrit Smith"). Evans proposed that Smith work to achieve passage of a bill that would make western lands free to homesteaders as a first step toward establishing a Republic based on universal land ownership. Smith did eventually support the NRA's bill, but he also responded to Evans by accusing him of harboring a deep-seated racism that prevented him from clearly appraising the relative conditions of the black slave and the white laborer. As David Roediger argues, Evans's narrow focus on the material comfort of the black slave and white wage worker inhibited a more comprehensive critique of wage labor. Evans's comparison focuses solely on economic relations between laborer and capitalist. To see the wage laborer as more oppressed than the slave he had to overlook the slave's political disenfranchisement and social death; consequently, he also overlooked the political and social dimensions of industrial exploitation.

Evans's simplistic view of slavery—and his view was far more generous and considered than those of other working-class leaders—can be explained by his racism. He actively discouraged Feargus O'Connor from supporting the American antislavery movement, publishing and distributing an open letter to the British Chartist leader. The letter claimed that Southern slavery was more palatable than Northern because the "barbarians of Africa" have "little of the pride or delicacy of the Caucasian." The white person's pride necessitated a broad "net" of social and cultural institutions in order to rationalize white slavery. This elaborate mechanism "hampers every fibre of his body and every faculty of his soul—a net of no one man's making, but the product of the ingenuity and villainy of ages" (A Member of the N.Y. Society for the Abolition of ALL Slavery). The pamphlet describes the distinction contemporary Foucauldian critics might make between a system of force and one of discipline. In the first case, direct physical force allows one class to dominate another. In the second, a broader cultural campaign secures the acquiescence or even approval of the oppressed class, making domination less visible and more intractable. Evans thus emphasizes the need for a powerful counter-hegemonic campaign to awaken white workers to their true condition.

As his attack on Smith indicates, Evans believed that the wage relationship enslaved the wage earner because the wage earner did not own the means of production. But Evans's appeal to small, self-employed artisans and his use of the term "white slavery," suggesting as it did that it was the whiteness of the wage worker that made his/her enslavement particularly unjust, led him ultimately to focus on the relative material conditions of slaves and wage workers, blunting his critique of the wage relationship.[12] Evans's proto-Marxist analysis became so ensnared in racial bigotry that it ended up harking back to a Jeffersonian America based on individual land ownership rather than projecting forward to an industrialized America that limited the destructive impulses of market capitalism.

The *Voice of Industry* also made comparisons between slavery and wage labor, but those comparisons stress similarities not only between Northern laborers and Southern slaves, but also between American industrial workers and Turkish slaves, medieval serfs and British wage laborers. In 1844–5, the editors do not suggest that antislavery reformers distract from labor reform more generally.[13] One description of "Anniversary Week" in Boston shows a coalition of reformers meeting to exchange information on organizing. The anonymous author of "Anniversary Week" describes, in glowing terms, the work of abolitionists, temperance reformers, and "workingmen" who have joined together "to work out a greater moral, physical and mental revolution than the world ever conceived of." The author eventually highlights the workingmen's efforts to combat all forms of slavery:

> The Workingmen have put on the whole armour, and entered the field of action—combating the powers of white, as well as black slavery—slavery

of avarice, want, half paid and oppressive toil; which is fast making us a nation of serfs, and transmitting to posterity a beggers [*sic*] inheritance.

("Anniversary Week")

This willingness to connect the plight of American industrial labor to other workers across race, nationality, and time may have its origins in the more utopian orientation of the paper. Unlike the narrower goals of the *Working Man's Advocate*, the *Voice of Industry* supported a variety of political reforms (legislation limiting working days to ten hours; a ban on child labor) as well as radical, socialist communities based on Charles Fourier's theories. Instead of the western township of (white) independent farmers envisioned by the *Working Man's Advocate*, the *Voice of Industry* described a socialist paradise of workers on a single, community-owned and operated complex of industry and farming. While such utopian communities proved short lived, they were important precursors to other publicly owned and operated ventures. The small, independent holdings envisioned by the NRA preserved a traditional, patriarchal social organization that was not adaptable to the increasingly large, complex operations necessary to an industrial nation.

The *Voice of Industry* was also more progressive in its stance toward women. It regularly published profiles of women working in a variety of industrial occupations, selling the entire collection of profiles under the title "Factory Tracts." The profiles were modeled on the British parliamentary reports on the condition of the laboring masses and similarly described abusive apprenticeship systems, poverty wages, and dangerous work conditions. Reflecting the importance of Lowell factory workers in supporting the paper, the *Voice* moved its headquarters from Fitchburg, Massachusetts, to Lowell and carried many articles excoriating the corporation owners and their lackeys for the exploitative conditions under which women worked in the mills.[14]

Despite the more inclusive rhetoric and Sarah Bagley's presence on the editorial board of the *Voice of Industry*, it still conveyed a conservative view of women's role in labor organizations. Bagley sought influence not only in the Female Labor Reform Association, of which she was president in 1845, but also within the New England Workingmen's Association. Her participation in one meeting at which she presented a banner sewn by the Female Labor Reform Association for the New England Workingmen's Association was summarized in the *Voice* as follows:

The presentation of Banner by Miss Sarah G. Bagley, and her address, which we copy below, were transactions of no small moment and importance, and doubtless will long be remembered by all present on that occasion. The banner with one or two trivial exceptions was beautiful and chaste . . . W.H. Channing replied in a brief, feeling and appropriate manner—showing woman's influence in past ages, in cheering and encouraging the hearts of humanities [*sic*] warriors, and strewing their rugged paths with flowers of consolation.

("New England Workingmen's Association")

Like the *Lowell Offering* writers, the *Voice of Industry* reporter goes to great lengths to defend female factory workers against any suggestion that they may be promiscuous, describing even the products of their hands as "chaste." But the writer also endorses Channing's view of women activists as cheerleaders. Bagley's own remarks recommended a much less ornamental role for women: "For the last half a century, it has been deemed a violation of woman's sphere to appear before the public as a speaker; but when our rights are trampled upon and we appeal in vain to legislators, what shall we do but appeal to the people?" ("New England Workingmen's Association") Couched in the terms in which feminist-abolitionists defended their right to public speech, Bagley's speech likewise insisted that women workers were not adequately represented by men.

A survey of the stories included in the *Voice of Industry* shows why women needed to control the representation of themselves. Despite the exposé of women's working conditions in "Factory Tracts," the fictional representations of "Woman" still offered an idealized view of the ever-patient, passive, apolitical woman. The author of "The Truant Husband" counsels women, "Had his wife met him with frowns and sullen tears, he had become a hardened libertine; but her affectionate caresses, the joy that danced in her sunken eye, the hectic flush that lit up her pallid cheek at his approach, were arguments that he could not withstand." The patient wife communicates with her body—her sunken eye and pallid cheek— the suffering she is prohibited from vocalizing. In another classic paean to the "angel in the home," the author contrasts such self-denying creatures to "a different class who prate of 'women's rights'" ("The Duty of Wives"). Bagley could speak on behalf of women as workers, but not critique their conventional role as wives.

Both the *Voice of Industry* and the *Working Man's Advocate* avoided characterizing women workers as promiscuous or vulnerable to sexual predators in the workplace, a characterization common in middle-class novels like *Les Miserables* and *A Tale of Two Cities*, the penny papers, or the writings of middle-class reformers like Orestes Brownson and the authors of the British parliamentary reports on the laboring classes. The subjects of sexual exploitation, women's greater independence from the sexual restraints of family and community in factory settings, or even the marriagability of factory women are never broached in either paper, not even in the veiled terms the *Lowell Offering* writers used. The *Voice of Industry* subscribed to a conventional, middle-class Victorian perception of women. Critics have claimed that the *Lowell Offering* lacked a sense of working-class consciousness, but other working-class papers did no better in fostering a sense of working-class agency among women.[15] These papers offered up an image of working-class women that merely reiterated the middle-class, Victorian belief that women's power emanated from their disembodied spirituality and their ability to rise above corporeal needs or desires. The papers' idealization of women's nature made effective organizing by women on behalf of their own material needs practically impossible. On the other hand, the *Lowell Offering*'s examination of women making vital choices did foster this agency.

Unlike the male writers for the *Voice of Industry*, the writers for the *Lowell Offering* critiqued this idealization of spiritually superior, undemanding women who relied on unspoken suffering to influence men. The story "Woman's Influence," discussed earlier, is an excellent example of this strategy; it counsels women to treasure their spiritual superiority, to remind men of it, but also to strike out independently if their men reject their "influence," a woman's version of "speak softly and carry a big (walking) stick."

All three of these working-class publications avoided critiques of industrialization that characterized workers as degraded brutes. Such characterizations were as likely to result in a rejection of workers as a reform of exploitative conditions. Defending her decision to publish positive portrayals of factory women, Farley wrote, "Still we might have portrayed the evils of a manufacturing system, had it not been a picture so often presented to the public . . . something surely was needed to counteract the false impression made by others" (Ella, "Conclusion of the Volume" 377). The Lowell mill women, nevertheless, found space to discuss the intersection of women's sexuality, pleasure, and work.

Female factory workers writing for the *Lowell Offering* resisted the work discipline of the mills by defending their right to pleasures, beauty, and self-culture. They repeatedly denounced the excessive rationalization of work. The author-narrator of one story details the ways in which a variety of women spend their leisure hours, rebuking those who spend their free time making extra money by sewing. Their greedy focus on production and accumulation, she claimed, was as reprehensible as spending money foolishly or reading trashy novels (D.). Another author takes a hardworking, big-eating farm family to task because it had become contemptuous of Mary, the one daughter educated by her genteel aunt to love reading and appreciate pretty home furnishings. A concerned neighbor counsels Mary's sister, "I cannot think it the duty of any one to labor entirely for the meat that perisheth" (A. F. D. 132).

In the most interesting treatment of this theme, "Aunt Letty; or, the Useful," the narrator Kate has a nightmare that her aunt's utilitarian spirit rules both natural and social spheres. The young, free-spirited girl describes her Aunt Letty as an old maid who

> was a pattern of industry, which the censorious might have termed the spirit of avarice. She was saving and prudent; always looking out to be prepared for a wet day. The uncharitable might have said she was so anxious to be ready for the storm, that she never allowed herself to enjoy the sunshine.
>
> (Kate 25)

The nightmare begins with Kate's lament that her beautiful flower garden has been transformed into a more useful vegetable garden. Nature becomes hyper-productive—the hens lay two eggs a day before dying of exhaustion, and a deluge of rain fosters the potato crop but ruins the hay. Nature's work speedup temporarily results in larger accumulations of capital, but such hyper-productivity ultimately turns back on itself, destroying the very raw materials necessary to continued production.

In the social realm, the narrator's father fires nearly all of their help, exhausting the remaining family members. As the avaricious spirit spreads, fully half of the town must migrate elsewhere in search of work. The narrator comments, "And I learned that all this toil, this sacrifice of social kindness, this narrowness of spirit, the blight of the beautiful, the absence of the ornamental, was not to meet the needs of man and animal nature; but to gain wealth, to acquire money. For what?" (27). The ultimate tendency of this focus on production is the commodification of people and the reification of gross matter or money. "Man, as a machine, might be kept at work until he wore out, and then, must be replaced with a new one . . ." (28). In a bid to escape this reduction to machine, the last hand on the farm marries Aunt Letty. But given Aunt Letty's willingness to work Kate to an early grave, Samuel's new family tie will likely have little effect on his fate. To show the ultimate tendency of Aunt Letty's utilitarian ethos, the narrator knits in church, the last remaining refuge from work. In an apocalyptic ending, the congregation converges on Kate before she wakes up from this nightmare.

As attacks on the Puritan work ethic, these stories teach that working to build stores of wealth does not demonstrate that one is of the Elect, but can sever one from all that is human or spiritual. An unbalanced focus on production—to the exclusion of pleasure, consumption, or reproduction (the reader can be sure that Aunt Letty and Samuel will not waste their productive energies on sex or children)—leads not to plenty but to death.

Because reformers' images of sexually promiscuous factory workers in Britain or sexually violated slave women stigmatized the very women that reformers hoped to help, working-class advocates almost always avoided depicting American women workers as sexual beings. The writers of the *Lowell Offering* recognized that their power as workers could be curtailed just as surely by being denied a right to appetites, including sexual appetite, as by being represented as reduced to appetite. If the woman worker lacked desires, then there would be no need to pay her more than a subsistence wage and no need to provide her with leisure hours. The mill women found in the de-sexualized woman worker another way of expressing their fears regarding machine culture.

Harriet Farley more explicitly showed the ultimately life-denying force of machine culture in her editorial response to the suicides of two operatives. One woman, with "no parents or home," had grown isolated and despaired of any change in her daily round of activities. While her body seemed to conform to the machine's regimen, her spirit, Farley says, revolted. "Day after day brought the same wearisome round of duties... The physical laws of her nature had not been violated, and nature still resisted the spirit's call for death" ("Editorial: Two Suicides" 214). Farley describes this woman's demise in unmistakably sexual terms:

> How heavily must life weigh upon her who flees to death for refuge!—who waits not for the grim tyrant, but rushes impetuously into his loathsome embrace!... and, when the innate delicacy of her nature is so far forgotten that the body, itself, is yielded up to the cold eye, and unshrinking hand, of the dissector—for this must always follow. (213)

The sterility of the factory seems a "violation" of her spirit, which craves social interaction. The young woman prefers a death described in terms of a ravishing embrace by "the grim tyrant" and the dissector.

The female factory operatives tended to be well-fed, well-dressed, and well-housed. They were materially comfortable, primarily because they were single and few had dependents. They could sustain themselves, however, only if they continued to be relatively isolated. The sterility of this life contrasted sharply with more common depictions of industrial cities teaming with subhuman workers—an image that began in the penny papers, was perpetuated in the mystery novels of Eugene Sue and George Lippard, and became best known in the middle-class novels of Rebecca Harding Davis, Victor Hugo, and Charles Dickens. This image of a mechanized and sterile economic order might have served better as a means of mobilizing workers than the gritty realism developing out of the penny papers.

If in the family protection campaign, abolitionists showed how slavery brutalized all who participated in the system, reducing humans to their physicality, the *Lowell Offering*'s stories of over-rationalization showed how an unchecked market logic could reduce humans to their productive capacities and eventually to mere abstractions. The mechanized worker was really the opposite end of the spectrum from the slave on the block. In all but the antislavery press, the slave on display was advertised as strong and fertile, but denied intellectual or emotional qualities. The pale, exhausted factory girl, on the other hand, since she was not a form of capital like the slave, required no reproductive capacity or self-sustaining strength to serve mill owners.

For the female slave, exploitation derived from her too-visible, too-sexual body. The female factory worker, on the other hand, ran the risk of being reduced to the level of machine, her sexuality completely submerged and her physicality valued only insofar as it was appended to machinery. While the writers for the *Lowell Offering* complained of exhausting work and, very occasionally, low pay, they reserved their greatest ire for the bell that signaled the beginning and end of the workday as well as meal breaks. Being compelled to respond to a bell subordinated the women to their machines and called forth some of the most direct comparisons between factory women and slaves. In one story designed to chip away at the social stigma factory women faced, a character hostile to the factory women describes them as follows: they are "driven like slaves, to and from their work, for 14 hours in each day, and dare not disobey the calls of the factory bell" (Ethelinda, "Prejudice Against Labor" 136). In a similar story, another character says, "There are objections to factory labor, which serve to render it degrading—objections which cannot be urged against any other kind of female employment. For instance, to be called and to be dismissed by the ringing of a bell, savors of compulsion and slavery" ("Factory Labor" 199).

The *Lowell Offering*'s use of machine metaphors for female factory workers presaged end-of-the-century naturalism. Among the only other place we find such tropes in antebellum writing are in Melville's bleak stories, *Bartleby the Scrivener* and *The Paradise of Bachelors and the Tartarus of Maids*. The other scriveners in Bartleby's office are imperfect workers because they do not conform to machine-like regularity. Their copying work is marred by their desires and appetites; Turkey overeats at midday and, with an excess of energy, recklessly blots documents. Nippers suffers from "two evil powers—ambition and indigestion," causing outbursts of temper (16). Unlike the other two scriveners, Bartleby conforms to machine culture. He initially seems to "gorge himself" on documents, consuming little else, writing "silently, palely, mechanically" (19, 20). He is beyond the equivalencies of market culture, refusing to spend his earnings or even eat the bare minimum to sustain himself. Consuming papers rather than food, annihilating the desires and appetites that impaired his coworkers, Bartleby eventually ceases all activity and begins wasting away.

In *The Paradise of Bachelors and the Tartarus of Maids*, Melville elaborates on this theme of the worker reduced to machine and then consumed in the process of production, adding a commentary on gender. The narrator visits a men's club where wealthy gentlemen conspicuously consume vast quantities of food and drink. Without wives and children, this "fraternal" band is free to travel and indulge themselves. They stand in stark contrast to the rooted, pale "maids" of the paper mill where the narrator next visits. Like Bartleby staring absently at the blank wall of his Wall Street office, these "pale" maids merge with the pale paper they make, the narrator speculates, from the rags of the bachelors. "At rows of blank-looking counters sat rows of blank-looking girls, with blank, white folders in their blank hands, all blankly folding blank paper" (328). Overseen by "Old Bach," they serve their machines "cringingly as the slave serves the Sultan" (328). The female workers exist on the detritus of bachelors' lives, attending not only their machines but their severe employer, himself a well-fed, well-dressed bachelor. He personifies the "iron animal," the machinery that first transforms these women into blank parchment and then annihilates them. The paradise of bachelors and tartarus of maids are not merely counterparts, but mutually dependent on one another. The virgins of the mill engender and support Old Bach, and by extension all of the fraternal band of wealthy capitalists. They, in turn, subsist on the bachelor's castoffs, in a cycle, not of reproduction, but of extinction reminiscent of Kate's nightmare in "Aunt Letty; or, the Useful."

Mark Seltzer calls this double movement, this shift both toward the body and its dissolution, "dematerialized materialism:"

> What from one point of view appears as the reduction of persons and actions to sheer physicality or materiality, appears, from another, as the abstraction of bodies, individuals, and "the natural" itself.
>
> (*Bodies and Machines* 14)

Although Seltzer locates this tension between market and machine culture in end-of-the-century cultural forms, particularly the naturalist novel, it is important to note that the writers for the *Lowell Offering*, and later Rebecca Harding Davis and Herman Melville, anticipated this tension. Where critics have dismissed the *Lowell Offering* for having insufficient working-class consciousness, they have overlooked the larger cultural criticism implicit in the tropes and narratives of the paper.

Not only do Melville and the writers for the *Lowell Offering* share a common critique of market culture as it morphed into machine culture, but they similarly reject the common imagery of hyper-sexualized factory women. Melville's "maids" are virgins, their mill compared to a convent. With the exception of the coded seduction story, "History of a Hemlock Broom," there is not one representation of a "fallen" woman in the *Lowell Offering*. On the contrary, there are stories in which women are falsely accused, and the narrator reprimands women's failure to stand together as "sisters."[16] Working against common representations of factory women as abandoned and degraded, these early critiques of machine culture more frequently represent them as stripped of all vitality, especially sexuality.

Compared with male-edited working class newspapers, the *Lowell Offering* stands out for the scope of its critique; it exposed not only the exploitation of workers, but the inhumanity of emerging scientific rationality that reduced humans to not only commodities, in the case of slaves, but machines, in the case of factory workers. The writers for the *Lowell Offering* built upon the antislavery family protection campaign by casting a critical look at the lack of freedom women experienced on family farms. Like E.D.E.N. Southworth, they found the tropes of antislavery a useful way to represent women's domestic lives, but unlike Southworth their identification with slaves did not take the form of making invidious comparisons.

PART 3

THE END OF ANTISLAVERY SENTIMENTALITY

CHAPTER 6

FREDERICK DOUGLASS'S POST-CIVIL WAR PERFORMANCE OF MASCULINITY

A character which [*sic*] might pass without censure as a slave cannot so pass as a freeman. We must not beg men to do for us what we ought to do for ourselves. The prostrate form, the uncovered head, the cringing attitude, the bated breath, the suppliant, outstretched hand of beggary does not become an American freeman, ...

(Douglass, "The Color Question" 420)

> I, too, sing America.
> I am the darker brother.
> They send me to eat in the kitchen
> When company comes,
> But I laugh,
> And eat well,
> And grow strong.
> Tomorrow,
> I'll be at the table
> When company comes.
> Nobody'll dare
> Say to me,
> "Eat in the kitchen,"
> Then.
> Besides,
> They'll see how beautiful I am

And be ashamed–
I, too, am America.
Langston Hughes, "I, Too"

Before the Civil War, Frederick Douglass masterfully drew upon the abolitionist family protection campaign in his autobiographies, speeches, and
articles. As a fugitive slave, he testified to the brutality of slavery: it had
severed his bond with his mother, left him unacknowledged by his white
father, and subjected his Aunt Hester to the violence of a jealous overseer.
His autobiographies are peopled by the stock characters of the family protection campaign: the fatally beautiful slave woman; the lustful driver; the
loving, traumatized slave mother; and the brutal slave mistress who vio-
lates the principles of true womanhood. He repeatedly inveighed against
the practice of separating families in his speeches. This 1855 speech is
just one example: "Every slaveholder claims the right to sell his slaves,
who, having local attachments, families, wives and little ones . . . can be
kept in submission by the threat of a sale and separation from all these"
("An Inside View of Slavery" 9). Douglass provoked his audience's fear
of loss, stoked it until he produced tears, and then used it to stimu-
late a loathing of slavery. He was an expert at the use of antislavery
sentimentality.

In his post-War speeches, however, Douglass made an intentional shift
in rhetorical strategies, away from the family protection campaign and
toward a celebration of African American masculinity, using the tropes of
the black soldier and the self-made, signifying man as models for African
American advancement. In his speeches, Douglass himself performed this
new strategy, using humor, irony, and personal anecdotes to offer himself, as a biracial American, as a rebuttal to reactionary arguments against
interracial cooperation.

Douglass's rhetoric shifted in response to three crucial developments.
First, throughout the 1850s, Douglass drew away from the Garrisonians
and their policy of nonresistance. He promoted electoral politics and a
new, more militant rhetoric, premised on confrontation rather than martyrdom. Second, following the Civil War, Douglass recognized the new
challenges facing African Americans and directly commented upon the
shortcomings of the family protection campaign. The family protection
campaign inspired revulsion from white Northerners who read sensation-
alized depictions of how slavery undermined marriage and parenthood
in the South. This response was useful to abolitionists hoping to end the
institution of slavery, but the campaign could inspire revulsion of not only
slavery but also African Americans, who might have seemed irredeemably
damaged by slavery. After the Civil War, Douglass disseminated new

tropes and narratives to promote a free labor society that fully included African Americans.

Third, the break between the (white) women's movement and the African American civil rights movement over the Fifteenth Amendment sundered the alliance that had formed the family protection campaign in the first place. Despite Douglass's long-term devotion to women's rights, he believed that the Fifteenth Amendment would not pass if it gave women as well as black men the vote. He argued that it was imperative to pass the amendment right after the Civil War while Americans still felt strongly about empowering African Americans. He made the vote the final step in ending slavery and protecting the integrity of the black family:

> When women, because they are women, are hunted down through the cities of New York and New Orleans; when they are dragged from their houses and hung upon lamp-posts; when their children are torn from their arms, and their brains dashed out upon the pavement; when they are objects of insult and outrage at every turn; when they are in danger of having their homes burnt down over their heads; when their children are not allowed to enter schools; then they will have an urgency to obtain the ballot equal to our own.
>
> ("We Welcome the Fifteenth Amendment" 216)

These are sensational images, images foregrounding the need for black men to have the vote in order to protect their wives and children. Restoring the black family necessitated the vote for Douglass, but following the triumph of the Fifteenth Amendment, he ceased to disseminate images of black patriarchs unable to protect their families. Central to Douglass's attempts to suture free labor ideology to the empowerment of African Americans was the image of the successful, rising black patriarch.

I focus lastly on Frederick Douglass because he was a central figure among abolitionists and fully immersed in abolitionist discourse. He was the most popular speaker on the antislavery lecture circuit,[1] and a man still in his prime at the end of the Civil War. At a time when many of his partners in the movement turned away to pursue competing political interests and others retired in the hope that their work was done, Douglass continued the tradition of agitating for full African American citizenship.[2] Moreover, he traveled extensively, giving him ample opportunity to study and comment upon the wage labor system in the North and abroad. The Reconstruction era was a period of opportunity for African Americans and of personal optimism for Douglass. As Waldo E. Martin, Jr. has aptly described Douglass, he was a "liaison between influential whites and the black community" whose mission was to change the hearts and minds of the dominant culture and whose most powerful tool was his own representative life (55). Self-presentation was crucial.

I am concentrating upon Douglass's speeches written from the end of the Civil War until the end of Reconstruction for several reasons. First, Douglass's post-War autobiographies tended to be crafted to explain his past decisions, especially those that embroiled him in controversies. They were only secondarily concerned with shaping public policy or perceptions. His shorter journalistic pieces were certainly concerned with shaping public policy, but were also, by necessity, narrowly focused on immediate events. His speeches, by contrast, permitted extended commentary on long-range issues and were crafted over several months: in the years between 1865 and 1877 Douglass delivered only a few original keynote lectures per year, often giving the same lecture at several places.

Furthermore, though Douglass primarily regarded himself as a speaker and public performer, his speeches have been neglected and underrated. In his introduction to essays on Douglass's autobiographies and novel, William L. Andrews laments early estimates of Douglass: "Douglass's fame rested for a long time on his reputation as a man of affairs, not a man of letters, and on his accomplishments as a great nineteenth-century orator, rather than on his achievement as a writer of enduring cultural and literary import to America" (2). Andrews assumes that the speeches are not, in and of themselves, literary and worthy of close study. He contends that white readers who regarded Douglass primarily as an orator were reluctant to view African Americans as self-conscious literary stylists (3). However, an examination of Douglass's post-War speeches demonstrate how carefully crafted and dramatically staged they were. If anything, having Douglass's famously powerful voice and impressive carriage behind them, they must have been performative tour de forces. John Stauffer notes that the appendix of *My Bondage and My Freedom*, containing six speeches and one public letter, is longer than the chapters detailing his "life as a free-man" (56). Stauffer persuasively concludes that Douglass chose to define himself as a freeman through his oratory: "Douglass presented himself as a performer, unadorned as it were, with a narrative framework. He arranged the speeches chronologically so that readers could glimpse the evolution of this public persona" (Stauffer 56). By focusing on these remarkable performances, we gain a greater sense for Douglass's resourceful, improvisational approach to the limitations of the dominant discourses of his day.

My objective is not to analyze Douglass's political strategy during Reconstruction but to analyze his rhetorical and performative decisions. Waldo E. Martin, Jr., and William S. McFeeley admirably demonstrate how Douglass struggled to balance his loyalty to the Republican Party with his awareness of the party's compromises with reactionary forces during Reconstruction. Martin admits that "the Republican Party's betrayal of the Negro" in 1876 was "beyond the influence of any one person, regardless of his personal power" (82), and Douglass's editorship of the *New National Era* between 1870 and 1872 show him time and again drawing attention to Southern "barbarism" and calling for federal intervention to stop a host of antiblack practices: lynching, destroying black and white schools, persecuting teachers, mobbing Northern emigrants, stifling free speech, failing to enforce laws equally, and cheating sharecroppers. But the caution and decorum of Douglass's journalism stand in stark contrast with the daring and drama of his speeches. These electrifying performances, in which Douglass took on a multitude of voices and roles, were perfectly pitched to maximize his influence over the perception of African Americans in the dominant culture and to advance their interests. These Reconstruction Era speeches show a momentous shift in Douglass's representation of African Americans and his perception of the relationship between slavery and wage labor.

Douglass was a much sought after speaker throughout the Reconstruction Era, though he was challenged to find new ways of persuading listeners to support black civil and political rights. When he did bring back characters from the family protection campaign, he met with signal failure. For example, in May 1877, in the wake of the biggest setback yet to the cause, Douglass delivered a stinging attack on the myth of the Old Virginian, a patrician figure celebrated for his erudite and polished manners. Bitter at the federal government's withdrawal from the South, a withdrawal that formally ended Reconstruction and disenfranchised African Americans, Douglass briefly resuscitated his confrontational polemics of the antebellum era. He says of the Old Virginian,

> He is never in a hurry. In walking, his gait is slow, rather than measured, and his arms dangle, rather than swing in orderly union with the motion of his legs and body . . . . He has the sitting power of a Turk, and may be seen in his easy chair more hours in the day than any other man in America. He generally walks with a cane, often sits toying with a cane, and is seldom seen without a cane.
>
> ("Our National Capital" 459)

This speech disrupts the Lost Cause rhetoric celebrating the brotherhood of white soldiers from both the Union and the Confederacy, both sacrificing for their sense of home. Much like Charles Sumner's "Crime against Kansas" speech in the Senate,[3] this critical personification of a region resulted in a firestorm of criticism and calls for Douglass to step down as marshal for the District of Columbia. The old Virginian strikes one as the very reverse of Northern entrepreneurial energy, and references to the Turk and the cane suggest images of Saturnalian indolence. In the popular parlance of the day Turks had harems and regarded women as lambs, brought to the marital bed as to a slaughter.[4] The cane suggests both indolence and uncontrolled violence, provoking memories of Charles Sumner's beating with a cane following his "Crime against Kansas" speech. Like Sumner, Douglass characterizes antebellum Washington, D.C., as a "moral monster" with "contamination in its touch, poison in its breath, and death in its embrace" (456). Douglass dropped both the speech and the representation of the South from his repertoire following the uproar.

In fact, the triumph of free labor in the Civil War over slave labor meant that Douglass no longer found much benefit in pathologizing Southern families—white and black—in slave culture; in fact, it was counterproductive to do so since African Americans sought full citizenship by demonstrating their American-ness. It was necessary, however, to argue against a system of labor that continued to relegate African Americans to agricultural peonage. Douglass's rhetoric focused, thus, upon political and economic conditions in the South rather than social conditions. He argued that federal intervention was necessary to growing democracy and free labor in the South. To make this call for federal intervention consistent with notions of liberal democracy and unfettered labor contracts, he argued that to "Let the Negro Alone"—as one of his 1869 lectures was called—actually required federal protection of voting and civil rights: "My politics in regard to the negro is simply this: Give him fair play and let him alone, but be sure you give him fair play" ("Let the Negro Alone" 202). He elaborated,

> If you see a negro wanting to purchase land, let him alone; let him purchase it. If you see him on the way to school, let him go; don't say he shall not go into the same school with other people . . . If you see him on his way to the workshop, let him alone; let him work; don't say you will not work with him; that you will 'knock off' if he is permitted to work. (203)

Douglass reverses the logic that associated the free market with minimal government intervention, showing the necessity of the federal government's protection of free market institutions.

Douglass further emphasized this point later in 1869 by making his enterprising son, Lewis, his best example of talent wasted in the racial caste system. Lewis had been excluded from the Washington, D.C., Printers' Union on the basis of race, effectively ruining his chance to work in his profession. Douglass remarked, "I can more easily to-day [*sic*] enter my son in a law office in Rochester, than I can get him into a shipyard to help build ships. The reason is, that the higher you go up in the gradations of intelligence, the further you get from prejudice, the more reasonable men are" (203). The mass of African Americans struggling to find a place in the American economy were especially vulnerable to discrimination and needed protections, not only for their prosperity but for the country's prosperity, he argued.

Douglass increasingly linked African American citizenship in the South to economic growth in the area. The very things threatening to a slave society, he argued, were crucial to free society: free speech, access to education, and many small landholders rather than a few large plantation owners. Even technical innovation, a necessary element of industrial development, depended upon a more democratic and egalitarian society, he argued, remarking on not only the prosperity he found in the North upon fleeing slavery, but the technical advancements ("Which Greeley Are We Voting For" 306). All of these led to both greater aggregate wealth and more widespread prosperity.

Douglass maintained a delicate balance between this call for federal protections and his insistence on the conventional masculinity of black men and their courage, perseverance, and physical strength. The black soldier becomes the quintessential example, for Douglass, of an American self-made man, making the world in which he was to live free.[5] Douglass begins shortly after the Civil War to build upon this record of African American bravery in the Civil War, carefully balancing an image of the military hero with that of the peaceful citizen:

> Some things have been settled concerning my race, and one of the things settled is this, that the negro will fight. (Applause.) We have been accustomed to regard him as a natural born Christian (laughter)—so well born that he needed not to be born again; that if smitten on one cheek he would turn the other also; but the late war has decided that he would fight.
>
> ("We Are Here and Want the Ballot-Box" 129)

Douglass rejected the Uncle Tom image of African American masculinity as long suffering and even masochistic. He signifies on both Harriet Beecher Stowe's famous protest fiction, a work central to the family protection campaign but increasingly detrimental to African American civil rights, and the failure of many "Christian" slaveholders to baptize or offer religious instruction to their slaves. Douglass went on to defend the peacetime role of African Americans: "We shall not be sent away for another reason, because we are useful to you—useful to the South, useful to the

North, useful to the whole country. In time of peace useful as laborers, with whom in that Southern clime no laborers can compete, and
useful to you in time of war, because we can fight" (130). Anticipating
Booker T. Washington's "Atlanta Compromise," a speech designed to
solicit investment in the education and employment of African Americans in the South 30 years later, Douglass summarized, "The question
comes at once, shall the presence of this vast black population be made a
blessing to themselves and a blessing to us, a blessing to the whole country, or a curse to themselves, a curse to you, and a curse to the whole
country?" (130). Douglass constructs African Americans as a resource to
an enterprising nation. Moreover, he positions himself as a part of neither
the "vast black population" nor "you" but as part of "us," the "whole country." Rhetorically, he makes himself an advocate for the nation's interests
rather than black or white, Northern or Southern interests. The entire
nation profits by investing in black soldiers/citizens.

A corollary to this emphasis on the independent black soldier/citizen
was his rejection of philanthropy, which he regarded, rhetorically at least,
as counterproductive. He rejects "the prostrate form" of the suppliant and
the "outstretched hand of beggary," so reminiscent of common antislavery
depictions of Ethiopia with her arms outstretched, because they are "not
becom[ing] to the American freeman" ("The Color Question" 420).[6] He
concludes that black people "have been injured more than benefited by
the efforts of so-called benevolent societies" (420). Philanthropy had the
dangerous effect of creating dependency and, though Douglass does not
say so, undermining the image of masculinity that became central to his
post-Civil War campaign.

In performing this image of masculinity on the lectern, Douglass carefully injected humor with righteous indignation, satire with denunciation,
to break through to resistant white audience members while fostering
an image of traditional masculinity. In a forthrightly titled speech, "We
are Here and Want the Ballot-Box," delivered just after the end of the
Civil War, Douglass invoked and safely discharged fears of miscegenation: "And, so far as my own experience goes to show it, from the
peaceable manner in which the blood of the two races have [sic] lived
together for the last fifty years in this organism (Laughter)—I have not
the slightest fear of a war of races. (Loud laughter and applause.)" (127).
He would invoke these fears repeatedly and offer his own impressive
body—powerful, elegant, handsome—as proof of the desirability of racial
integration and intermarriage. Douglass frequently challenged audience
members' binary thinking on race by invoking his own complex background. In an 1872 speech delivered in Richmond, he classified himself
as one of the "poor white people" in the South:

Knowing that those States were free, that there were no slaves there, I expected to see the people living like we poor white people in the South that had no slaves lived. I include myself with you partly by permission and partly by circumstances over which I had no control. (Laughter.) I went up there expecting to find them living as we poor white people used to live, and you know some of you how that was—out on the outskirts of plantation, with a chimney built out of doors, not of brick, but a little wood, a little hay and a little clay. (Renewed laughter.) ("Which Greeley Are We Voting For?" *Frederick Douglass Papers* 304)

Before fleeing to the North as a fugitive slave, Douglass had worked in Baltimore's shipbuilding industry, selling his labor and handing over most of his wages to his owner. His Richmond, Virginia, audience members were likely surprised to be made visible, not as the opposition to Douglass, but as his compatriots glimpsing a new day in which Northern prosperity might come to the South. Douglass deconstructs the racial binary that labeled him as an unambiguously black man and that drew together slaveholding and poor white people. We find few of these playful references to his racial background in Douglass's antebellum speeches. Moreover, as editor of the *New National Era* between 1870 and 1872, he refers to himself exclusively as "a black man" ("The New Party Movement" 255) and to his constituency as "the colored men of the country" ("Salutatory of the Corresponding Editor" 220). His editorials are usually written in the first person plural, and this "we" always represents either black Americans or, more narrowly, the black men working on the paper. On paper, Douglass consistently played a single role—the eminent, high-minded editor.

However, Douglass's speeches, with their pauses for laughter and applause and with their frequent references to his own body, foreground the importance of not just his words but his physical presence amidst other physically performative bodies. The speeches were not so much spoken as acted, and audience members did not so much listen as participate in a call and response engaging their bodies in addition to their intelligence. Douglass created a sensation in 1866 among delegates—including many Northern governors, congressmen, and military officers—when he and white newspaper editor Theodore Tilton linked arms during a processional. Once they arrived at the hall where Union Loyalists met to organize against Andrew Johnson's antiblack policies, delegates clamored to hear Douglass. The *New York Herald* reported that "in spite of the efforts of the Chairman to obtain a hearing for other speakers, the universal desire was vociferously enforced, and amid deafening applause and cheering the dusky orator stepped on the rostrum...." ("We Are Here and Want the Ballot-Box," *New York Herald* 3).

Douglass's charisma among women was legendary. The *New York Herald* reported that at his "Let the Negro Alone" speech, delivered at the May 1869 American Anti-Slavery Society meeting, the platform included "a considerable number of colored ladies and a fair sprinkling of their white sisters" there to hear "the irrepressible Fred Douglass lionizing it to some extent among his anti-slavery brethren" (1). The *Concord Daily Monitor* remarked upon his drawing power during the 1870 presidential campaign:

> Phenix Hall was packed with the largest audience, last evening, ever gathered within its walls . . . . We have seen many large audiences gathered in the city in political campaigns in past years, especially during the years of the rebellion, but never such an audience as gathered last evening to greet Frederick Douglass, the eminent colored orator who has filled so conspicuous a place in the past.

The paper refers to his "satirization" of Democratic claims as "keen and effective" and his peroration as "electrical and thrilling" (2). When Douglass was introduced, he "was received with tremendous applause, and the waving of handkerchiefs by the hundreds of ladies present" (2).

Douglass had to be very careful in his rhetoric regarding racial mixing because increasingly the image of the black man desiring a white woman was used to justify political repression. The *Richmond Daily Monitor*, responding to his 1872 stump speech, "Which Greeley are We Voting For," remarked upon the "unusual" number of "the female sex of the colored race" and gave one of the most tepid reviews of Douglass found in the Reconstruction Era: "He spoke with ease and fluency, his gestures were appropriate, and his language well chosen, but as an orator he does not excel several well-known colored men in Virginia who were slaves until freed by the sword" ("A Big Grant and Wilson Meeting"). Clearly, the paper found both his charisma and aggressiveness, as evidenced by his decision to become a fugitive slave, threatening.

Douglass was aware of the delicate line he had to walk when it came to his self-presentation as neither submissive nor angry, neither bland nor sexually aggressive. He remarks on the development of the Ku Klux Klan as early as 1869:

> This third estate of Southern society [the KKK] is about as active and effective as any other class. They manage the midnight murders while members of the second class manage the electric wires, and issue all manner of lying excuses for their crimes. The standing excuse is, that some huge, ugly negro has insulted or outraged a white lady.
>
> ("We Are Not Yet Quite Free" 239)

The Ku Klux Klan had reversed the family protection campaign, making white womanhood rather than black womanhood endangered. Directly accusing white men of fabricating this attack on white women's honor would prove to be a risky strategy as newspaper presses were destroyed for such affronts.[7] Generally, Douglass chose more indirect methods of disrupting this rhetoric.

For example, in an 1875 stump speech for the Republican Party, Douglass satirized the Democrats' bogeyman of "social equality." One newspaper paraphrased the speech as follows:

> Another charge against the Republican party is that they have a bill pending in the Senate, to establish social equality. What is social equality? In what does it consist? Where does it begin and where does it end? He confessed he hardly knew. He knew what social inequality was, and had known it for a good while. They had a great deal of it where he came from. A great deal of the social, but no equality ... Out of that social inequality there had come a million and a half of intermediates. (Laughter and applause.)
>   ("New Hampshire for the Republicans" 405)

This personal display of biracial identity loosened up crowds and disrupted the growing power of the "second estate," those white newspaper editors fabricating images of black rapists stalking the Southern countryside, deflowering white womanhood. Fear of race riots and "social equality," a term that was read as synonymous with miscegenation in the parlance of the day, could be used to rally resistance to voting and civil rights for African Americans. Douglass uncouples miscegenation and civil rights by making visible the million and a half biracial people, himself among them, living in America. By posing as a naïf and positing rhetorical questions, Douglass encouraged white listeners to feel superior to the manipulative white supremacists who disingenuously suggested that interracial sexual relations were either unusual or prevented by social inequality in the antebellum era. Social equality in the new Reconstruction Era would lead to peace, he claimed, now that the white man did not sleep "on the quivering heartstrings of his slaves" ("Recollections of the Anti-Slavery Conflict" 366).[8]

This assertion of peaceful *interracial* feelings, however, did not imply post-war *sectional* harmony. He waved the bloody shirt on a number of occasions:

> If we ought to forget a war which has filled our land with widows and orphans, which has made stumps of men of the very flower of our youth, sent them on the journey of life armless, legless, maimed and mutilated; which has piled up a debt heavier than a mountain of gold—swept

uncounted thousands of men into bloody graves—and planted agony at a
million hearthstones; I say if this war is to be forgotten, I ask in the name of
all things sacred what shall men remember? ("The Unknown Dead" 291).

Douglass tried to disrupt the powerful discourse of white brotherhood
that grew up in the wake of the Civil War, a brotherhood emblematized by
popular renditions of the handshake between Generals Lee and Grant at
the South's surrender at Appomattox. Popular writers like Thomas Dixon
developed Confederate romances depicting the Civil War as a fratricidal
conflict healed by the marriage of (white) North and South and their
mutual defeat of African Americans. Douglass insisted on remembering
the conflict as one between freedom and tyranny and not as the "lost
cause" for which noble Confederates died.

Part of this campaign of disruption involved signifying on the familial
connections between black and white Southerners rather than between
whites North and South. Douglass did this with references to his own
body, but also by gently introducing the topic of miscegenation, sometimes with humor as above, but often more insistently and seriously. In
one of his most dramatic and successful speeches, "Let the Negro Alone,"
he appeared to shift loyalties, expressing sympathy for his "Democratic
brethren" who "have always been logical" and "seen a little further than
the Abolitionists themselves" (204). Addressing a convention celebrating the thirty-sixth anniversary of the American Anti-Slavery Society,
Douglass built suspense by seeming to side with those opposed to the
Fourteenth Amendment:

> I say I have sympathy for my Democratic friends when they say to me
> "Douglass, that is all right enough, but we see where it leads." They do see
> where it leads. Mr. Hendricks, on the floor of the Senate, said, "Gentlemen,
> this thing, suffrage for the blacks, is impossible, for it means the bringing
> of a black Senator into this House, to be seated in one of these chairs; it is
> impossible." He was right; it means all that, and I am just the man that is
> coming. (Laughter and applause.) (205)

Once again, Douglass pointed to his own physical presence and the
prospect of it occupying a seat in Congress.

He built on this mock dialogue between Democrats and former abolitionists, insisting that racial intermarriage could and should be encouraged: "The Democrat said, 'The right to vote means amalgamation.' The
Abolitionist said, 'No, that don't follow.' 'It will dissolve the Union.' 'No
it won't.' 'It will lead to amalgamation.' 'No, it won't.' But it will lead
just there. Don't be afraid" ("Let the Negro Alone" 205). Mimicking the

voices of the abolitionist and the Democrat allowed Douglass to cast the debate as a simplistic spat between children, one he authoritatively ended by defying both. As Granville Ganter remarks, Douglass "use[d] humor as a means of mastery, incorporating the discourse of his opponents and laughing derisively at them" (545). Douglass went on to insist that African Americans were already "under your arm," a figure of speech suggesting the embrace of a parent for a child. Significantly, Douglass was the son of a white man.

Repeatedly, Douglass insisted on the American-ness of African Americans. Taking issue with a previous speaker praising the "distinctive" peculiarity of each race, he said, "I believe in imitation ... and I am going to imitate all the good I can and leave all the bad I find in the world" (206). Racial essentialization, assigning specific intellectual and behavioral characteristics to physiological characteristics, often served to relegate racial minorities to second-class citizenship. Douglass defended African Americans by contrasting African American integration and Native American separatism: "He dislikes your civilization, dislikes and distrusts you. It is not so with the Negro" (207). Douglass strategically ignored a tradition of black separatism to make this claim. He went on to use humor to invoke and then minimize cultural differences between the newly freed African Americans and white Americans:

> Where there are Methodists, the negro is a Methodist; where there are Baptists, he is a Baptist; where there are Quakers, he is not exactly a Quaker, because they do not make noise enough for him (laughter), but he wears at least a plain coat.... There is nothing left for you, but to incorporate him completely into the American body politic (208).

Douglass would address this issue of African American integration in the "national family" in a more serious and sustained tone in his powerful speech at the dedication of the Freedman's Monument to Abraham Lincoln in 1876. In Washington, D.C., before an audience including President Ulysses S. Grant, members of Congress, and the most significant black leaders of the Reconstruction Era, Douglass said,

> [Lincoln] was willing to pursue, recapture, and send back the fugitive slave to his master, and to suppress a slave rising for liberty, though his guilty masters were already in arms against the Government. The race to which we belong were not the special objects of his consideration.... We are at best only his step-children, children by adoption, children by force of circumstances and necessity.
>
> ("The Freedmen's Monument to Abraham Lincoln" 432)

One might say—though here Douglass would have overstepped the boundaries of acceptable public discourse—that African Americans were Lincoln's unacknowledged children. When Douglass said Lincoln was at times "wounded in the house of his friends," he was referring to a national house containing African Americans and abolitionists (437). Douglass did not care for the Freedman's Monument, designed by the German sculptor Thomas Ball, which depicted Lincoln raising up a kneeling and shackled male slave. However, the dedication gave him an opportunity to cast African Americans as the nation's Ishmael, an exile who deserved to be fully recognized by his unjust parent.[9]

Poet Langston Hughes would later memorialize the historical position of African Americans in the national polity as akin to that of the unacknowledged black child in his white father's household. African Americans are the "darker brother[s]," Hughes said, capable of "laughing" and "growing strong," because they see their segregation within both the family and the nation as temporary, to be defeated by the sheer charisma of the "darker brother." Douglass ventriloquized the voices of Democrats, Southerners, even cautious Republicans to marginalize their positions and to promote his own vision of a multiracial, free labor South. He offered his own biracial body as a representative American body—sometimes a poor white man, sometime a privileged outsider, sometimes a "darker brother." With humor and satire, Douglass sought to replace the stock images of tragic mulattas, Simon Legrees, and Uncle Toms with the more dignified images of the black soldier and self-made, signifying man. Through this exercise in impersonation, Douglass engaged his listeners in a paradigm shift.

Images of sturdy homes and patriotic families proliferate in Douglass's speeches. He warned that the Democrats would bring violence to the South but that "every victory of the Republican party helps to protect them [African Americans] in their little homes" ("New Hampshire for the Republicans" 406). Then he followed with a call to elect the party of Lincoln in repayment for the courage and sacrifice of African American soldiers: "When the cloud of battle lowered upon the country, and threatened to overwhelm us with defeat and disaster, Abraham Lincoln called upon the negro to advance; and they came 200,000 strong, to the defense of the flag" (406).

Compared with Lydia Maria Child, one of his fellow abolitionists who continued to write in the service of African American civil rights after the Civil War, Douglass did not use maternalist politics nor did he imagine an enlarged government apparatus as primarily maternal and protective. He saw this enlarged government as an extension, rather than compromise, of free labor ideology. A maternalist politics—imagining an enhanced government apparatus as a mother figure educating, leading, and protecting disempowered people—undermined the independent black worker at the center of Douglass's free labor ideology. Whereas Child chose reforms consistent with this political rhetoric, including her design of *The Freedmen's Book* to be used as a primer in the new schools for freed slaves, Douglass focused on protecting the vote and promoting a new image of the black soldier as antidote to the emasculated victim. It was Douglass, rather than Child, who led the new generation of civil rights activists post-Civil War and Douglass's new cluster of images and narratives that prevailed.

Douglass's perception of Southern labor relations compared with Northern "free labor" resembled that of the Lowell mill workers more than that of Lydia Maria Child. Following the Civil War, he saw more of a continuity between agricultural peonage and the worst forms of "cheap labor" in industrializing cities. An oversupply of labor drove down wages in the North and work conditions among sharecroppers in the South. Douglass's vision for the mass of African Americans relied upon their ability to stay in the South as a valuable work force and to bargain for better labor contracts or to work their own land as a means of improving their collective wealth, status, and direct political power. He did not envision a maternalist social field as a remedy, nor did he focus upon the "dangerously free" street child. Like the women workers writing for the *Lowell Offering*, he portrayed an image of thrifty, hardworking adults more than capable of sustaining themselves if not thrown into competition with an oversupply of workers and if treated equally before the law.

An 1871 editorial in the *New National Era* deconstructed the rhetoric of "cheap labor" as beneficial to the nation:

> Cheap labor is a phrase that has no cheering music for the masses. Those who demand it, and seek to acquire it, have but little sympathy with common humanity. It is the cry of the few against the many.... It is the deceitful cry of... the taper-figured dandy against the hard-handed working man.
>
> ("Cheap Labor" 264)

Douglass went on in this article to make the black laborer of the South the prime example of this "hard-handed working man," saying former slaveowners were soliciting immigrants "to be independent of their former slaves, and bring their noses to the grindstone" (265). In an editorial just two months later, entitled "The Labor Question," Douglass supported passage of a bill to investigate the wages, hours, and sanitary conditions of the laboring classes, including within this category Southern sharecroppers and predicting the measure would be "of especial advantage to colored labor," which was not "understood" (285). It was important to Douglass that black sharecroppers were understood to suffer as much from the land monopoly in the South as urban workers suffered from a monopoly of productive capital.

Douglass did still share much with Child, however. Like Child, who published a novel—*Romance of the Republic*—celebrating interracial families after the Civil War, he did not seek to uncouple "social equality" from interracial marriage, choosing instead to defend an image of African Americans as part of the national family; metaphorically, he offered his own biracial body as a representative American body. In his performance of his dual identity as self-made American and the "darker brother" fighting exclusion, Douglass engaged his listeners in a paradigm shift. Much of the power in Douglass's speeches come from this self-staging, an aspect of his work that has been lost to many contemporary readers.

Antislavery sentimentality and the family protection campaign—of which Douglass and Child were such central spokespeople—succeeded in linking slavery to a host of anti-family practices: separating children from parents, destroying slave marriages, raping slave women, undermining the "true womanhood" of slave mistresses, and converting slaveholding men into tyrants. As a strategy for African American advocacy post-Civil War, however, it was limited. Douglass's cluster of images and his performance as representative black man dovetailed with the political turn toward the "labor question" as well as the literary turn toward realism and away from sentimentality. It was Douglass's new image of the American body politic and his speaking performances that would inspire the Civil Rights movement in the 1950s and 1960s.

NOTES

INTRODUCTION

1. See Ellen DuBois's groundbreaking essay, "Women's Rights and Abolition: The Nature of the Connection"; Jean Fagan Yellin's *Women and Sisters: The Antislavery Feminists and American Culture*; and Karen Sanchez-Eppler's *Touching Liberty: Abolition, Feminism, and the Politics of the Body*.
2. Nancy F. Cott says of the Second Great Awakening (1798–1830s), "Conversion set up a direct relation to God's authority that allowed female converts to denigrate or bypass men's authority—to defy men—for God" (21). See "Young Women in the Second Great Awakening in New England."
3. For example, Harriet Beecher Stowe published a particularly inflammatory statement by a well-known clergyman in Chapter 12 of *Uncle Tom's Cabin*. Dr. Joel Parker excused slavery by saying that the evil practices found in it were the same as evil practices one might find in marriage, parenting, or other forms of employee-employer relations. Singled out for calumny in the best-selling book of its era, Dr. Parker sued Stowe for libel. A dispute raged in the pages of the *New York Observer*, a pro-slavery religious paper, provoking Dr. Parker to characterize Stowe as "unladylike" for engaging in such "coarse" debates (227). See Joan D. Hedrick's *Harriet Beecher Stowe: A Life*, 225–32.
4. Raymond Williams elaborates upon Antonio Gramsci's definition of hegemony, describing a belief as hegemonic if it is so deeply embedded in a culture that it escapes close examination and becomes "common sense." The belief that slavery undermined the family and led to the abuses detailed in antislavery writings was an emergent and contested belief in the 1830s, but following Stowe's *Uncle Tom's Cabin*, that belief became increasingly hegemonic. See *Marxism and Literature*, 108–14.
5. I use the term "counter-hegemonic" to describe the Garrisonians' use of elements of the dominant culture to push an agenda hostile to prevailing economic structures. Antonio Gramsci's concept of hegemony is particularly relevant in this context because it avoids any totalizing theory of culture as the effect of necessary economic developments. Gramsci uses the term "hegemony" to describe the cultural activity that secures the nation's consent to the current economic structures. For Gramsci, such superstructural activities, the domain of civil society, are not at all separate from economic structures or from the state but are in fact integral to both. Gramsci describes two superstructural "levels." One level occurs in civil society through the

operation of the dominant class. This is hegemony. The other superstructural level occurs in the state, using essentially negative means to codify
and enforce the cultural norms of the dominant class. The state uses "direct
domination" to discipline those groups who do not "consent" to the cultural
norms of the dominant class. Counter-hegemonic movements use elements
of dominant culture that can be "rearticulated" to contribute to alternative
views of economic and political organizations. See especially *Selections from
the Prison Notebooks*, 12–13.

6. See David Roediger, *The Wages of Whiteness*.

7. See Herbert Shapiro, "Labor and Antislavery: Reflections on the Literature"; Edward Magdol, *The Antislavery Rank and File*; Eric Foner, *Politics
and Ideology in the Age of the Civil War*; John Ashworth, *Slavery, Capitalism,
and Politics in the Antebellum Republic*; and especially the debate between
David Brion Davis, John Ashworth, and Thomas L. Haskell in the *American
Historical Review* 92.4.

8. See James Oakes' *Slavery and Freedom: An Interpretation of the Old South*.
Oakes writes, "What little statistical evidence we have indicates that as many
as one in three slave families in the South was broken by the force of
the master—suggesting that perhaps 600,000 slave families were shattered
between 1820 and 1860" (9). Oakes goes on to note that unlike other New
World slave societies, American slave society in the nineteenth century with-
drew from the slave trade and had a balanced sex ratio. "And most tragic of
all, because a balanced sex ratio allowed American slaves to create a family
life for themselves, the consequences of their legal kinlessness were uniquely
appalling. For it made the disruption and breakup of slave families one of
the endemic features of slavery in the American South" (35).

9. Stephanie Coontz argues that the pace at which production shifted out of the
home peaked between 1815 and 1840. Furthermore, Americans understood
that the factory system, in which production occurred outside of the home
and workers did not own or control the means of production, was the "wave
of the future" (164).

10. See George M. Frederickson, "Uncle Tom and the Anglo-Saxons: Romantic
Racialism in the North," and Marianne Noble, *The Masochistic Pleasures of
Sentimental Literature*.

11. In just one of many examples, in *Sweet Love's Atonement* and its sequel, *Zenobia's Suitors*, slave owners twice try to pass the Spanish Zenobia off as a slave,
and both light-skinned, female slaves in the novels are sold away from their
families by close relatives (a foster mother and a son).

CHAPTER 1

1. See David Brion Davis, *The Problem of Slavery in Western Culture*.

2. See Sanchez-Eppler, *Touching Liberty*, 4–8. Under pressure from antislavery and feminist movements, Americans were forced to examine just which
"persons" were entitled to the rights granted by the Bill of Rights and to

include racially and sexually explicit language into the Constitution. Prior to 1865, a white, male identity was implicitly assumed. See also Nancy Bentley's analysis of the body of the "white slave" in "The Mulatto Hero in Antebellum Fiction" *Subjects & Citizens: Nation, Race, and Gender from Oroonoko to Anita Hill*, 195–216. Bentley writes, "The tacit rules of the domestic novel ... are these: for women's bodies and black bodies the infliction of violence or abuse can be a means by which the individual achieves a transcendent grace or enriched dignity and identity ... But the idea that violence to a white man's body would enhance his selfhood is nonsensical or heretical—despite the fact that the model for the passive power of martyrdom, Jesus Christ, was a white man" (196). Liberation for the black slave—and for women—in antebellum fiction often takes a spiritual form and requires the body's humiliation and destruction.

3. See Michel de Certeau, *The Practice of Everyday Life*.
4. I am indebted here to Augusta Rohrbach's work, *Truth Stranger Than Fiction: Race, Realism and the U.S. Literary Marketplace*. Augusta Rohrbach, argues that antislavery literary culture brought together the humanitarian narrative, the rise of print culture, and industrial capitalism in a potent mix anticipating American literary realism. The humanitarian narrative depicts bodily suffering along with a strong injunction to stop such suffering. This narrative is premised on the idea that literature can and should play a powerful role in social reform. Moreover, she argues that antislavery literature, especially slave narratives and Garrison's paper *The Liberator*, pressured readers to commit their money to their morals by juxtaposing antislavery stories and advertisements for antislavery commodities, pioneering the first commercial "tie-ins" in newspapers. Accounts in slave narratives of the importance of fund-raising to future efforts to liberate slaves further encouraged antislavery consumption.

CHAPTER 2

1. Lydia Maria Child, *Letters from New York*. Hereafter cited parenthetically as *LNY*. When I am referring to the column as it first appeared I place the title in quotation marks. When I refer to the collected letters, from which my quotes are taken, I italicize the book title.
2. The body of this chapter refers exclusively to those letters published in the *National Anti-Slavery Standard*, most of which were collected in the first edition of *Letters from New York*. Those published in the second series primarily appeared in the *Boston Courier*, a more mainstream paper, after Child had stepped down from editing the *National Anti-Slavery Standard*. She declared her intention to focus upon refining her literary skills, and the letters are considerably less political, though one records a trip to Blackwell Island, one endorses temperance, and one defends the explicit representation of evils by antislavery, temperance, and prison reform movements. Generally, children appear in this second series as reminders of the innate goodness of human nature; Child seldom remarks upon their class position.

3. Seth Koven and Sonya Michel coined the term "maternalist politics" to describe the rhetoric and political tactics of major Progressive Era reforms led by women. These leaders argued that it was the special province of women and mothers to protect the weak. See Koven and Michel (eds.), *Mothers of a New World: Maternalist Politics and the Origins of Welfare States*.

4. See the debate between David Brion Davis, John Ashworth, and Thomas L. Haskell in *American Historical Review* 92 (4). Of special note here are Davis, "Reflections on Abolitionism and Ideological Hegemony," 797–812, and Haskell, "Convention and Hegemonic Interest in the Debate over Antislavery: A Reply to Davis and Ashworth," 829–78.

5. For an elaboration of Child's views on slave labor, wage labor, and the modern family, see John Ashworth, *Slavery, Capitalism and Politics in the Antebellum Republic* Vol. 1, 165–68.

6. See Jacques Donzelot, *The Policing of Families*; Christopher Lasch, *Haven in a Heartless World*; June Howard, *Form and History in American Literary Naturalism*; and Karen Sanchez-Eppler, "Playing at Class." Both Howard and Sanchez-Eppler argue that Progressive Era reformers (Howard) and Child (Sanchez-Eppler) cast themselves as sensitive observers, capable of both sympathy and systemic analysis, in comparison with the working class, who, because they were brutalized, required expert guidance. The social field, in their view, thus arose to inflate reformers' sense of self-importance and to protect the middle and upper classes from the "dangerous classes." Child's criticism of working-class isolation and her defense of Catholic schools—which taught children an alternative view of Catholicism and fought the Protestant bias in the mainstream curriculum—suggest she had a more generous estimate of the working class.

7. The most notorious woman Child helped and wrote about in the "Letters from New York" was Amelia Norman, a young, working-class woman who had been seduced by a wealthy man and then attempted to murder him when he abandoned her in a brothel. In the subsequent trial, Child championed Norman, publishing a defense of her in "Letters from New York," which, according to Margaret Fuller, was used by Norman's defense attorney to win her acquittal. Child expressly denied that economic motives might have propelled either Norman's choice in a lover or her decision to become a "kept" woman. Removing class from consideration of the dynamics between Norman and Ballard, Child made this seduction tale a paradigmatic story of gender relations but not of Northern economic and social relations. Child's ability to intervene through the press and the court took Norman's fate out of the private, familial realm within which the tragic mulatta and Southern white woman were trapped. In addition to helping Amelia Norman, Child helped actress Jeannie Barrett control her alcoholism and resume her acting career, and she championed murderer John C. Colt's alleged wife after he was executed. See Lydia Maria Child, "Uncollected Letter," 368 and 370. See also, Carolyn Karcher, *The First Woman in the Republic: A Cultural Biography of Lydia Maria Child*.

8. Recent scholarship has called into question the theory that the Industrial Revolution ushered in a rift between the public sphere and the domestic or private sphere for middle-class Americans. Critics have shown how the lived experience of men and women regularly defied the culturally prevalent notion that public and private spheres should be as separate as possible. Child's vision of feminine and masculine "souls" and her call for a more feminized public sphere makes her an appropriate example of Nina Baym's reframing of the ideology of separate spheres: "Public and private spheres were metaphorical rather than actual places[;] ... public and private were different ways of behaving in the same space" (*American Women Writers and the Work of History, 1790–1860*, 11). For more on this debate, see Alejandro Lugo and Bill Maurer (eds.), *Gender Matters: Rereading Michelle Z. Rosaldo*, and Monika M. Elbert (ed.), *Separate Spheres No More: Gender Convergence in American Literature, 1830–1930*.

9. Sanchez-Eppler argues that images of street children at play and "stories of street-children's vulnerability and pathos" operate in concert with one another to both justify the exploitation of children and let the sympathetic, middle-class viewer off the hook. She specifically cites Child's "Letters from New York" as an instance of middle-class paralysis toward working-class children. Her critique resembles Donzelot's insofar as she considers the development of the social field—in this case Charles Loring Brace's Children's Aid Society—primarily a means of disempowering the working class and containing more radical impulses. See Sanchez-Eppler, "Playing at Class," 838, 822, and Donzelot, *The Policing of Families*.

10. In *The Political Unconscious: Narrative as a Socially Symbolic Act*, Frederic Jameson uses the terms "magical narrative" and "imaginary resolution" to describe the operation of the romance genre. He argues that the romance provides an "imaginary resolution of the objective contradictions to which it thus constitutes an active response" (118). In Child's early fiction, there is a contradiction between the didactic tale she wished to tell, the tale of hard-working, virtuous young girls who earn their way out of poverty, and the reality of low wages and limited opportunities for women. Child magically resolves this contradiction by making these poor girls the sisters and wives of middle-class characters. They "earn" their upward mobility through virtuous behavior, defined according to a middle-class ethic of hard work and conformity, rather than wages. See "The Cottage Girl" and "Louisa Preston" in particular.

11. See Lydia Maria Child, *Lydia Maria Child: Selected Letters, 1817–1880*, hereafter cited parenthetically as *SL*.

12. See letters 14, 18, 29, 31, 32, 44. Letter 31, on the execution of John C. Colt, and her uncollected letter from February 6, 1844, on the trial of Amelia Norman, are of particular interest.

13. The Five Points neighborhood was created in the early nineteenth century when city forefathers arranged to have a fresh water pond filled in to expand living space. The resulting marshy land lacked bedrock, and soon the buildings on top of it began to sink and to become infested with disease-carrying

insects. See Tyler Anbinder, "We Will Dirk Every Mother's Son of You": Five Points and the Irish Conquest of New York Politics."

14. Child's portraits of Zeek, a clever fugitive slave, and his daughter, Julia Pell, a well-known evangelical preacher, attest to the creativity with which some poor city dwellers met severe challenges and developed full lives. See letter 11.

15. In 1830, Owen and Wright proposed a system of education in which the state would remove children from their homes and finance the education of all children in boarding schools. Housing children of the rich and the poor together would counter the negative effects of both poverty and excessive luxury, ennobling labor and reducing class stratification. See Richard William Leopold, *Robert Dale Owen: A Biography*, 87, 92–3.

16. Child's advice manual on child rearing, *The Mother's Book* (1831), also departs from similar works by the Abbotts and Beecher in its endorsement of communication and intimacy between parent and child and its corresponding de-emphasis on obedience and discipline. See David J. Rothman, *The Discovery of the Asylum: Social Order and Disorder in the New Republic*, 213–20, esp. 213–14.

17. The plight of New York's newsboys became a celebrated cause in the 1850s, a decade after Child's "Letters," when abolitionist Charles Loring Brace founded a home for orphaned newsboys. Brace was encouraged in his work with the Children's Aid Society by Frederick Law Olmsted, author of a famous indictment of slavery as an economic system, *The Cotton Kingdom*. Olmsted wrote to Brace in 1853, "Go ahead with the Children's Aid and get up parks, gardens, music, dancing schools, reunions which will be so attractive as to force into contact the good and the bad, the gentlemanly and the rowdy. And the state ought to assist these sort of things" (qtd. in Laura Wood Roper, *FLO: A Biography of Frederick Law Olmsted* 94).

18. Child writes, "That the law of Love may cheer and bless even public establishments, has been proved by the example of the Society of Friends. They formerly had an establishment for their own poor, in the city of Philadelphia, on a plan so simple and beautiful, that one cannot but mourn to think it has given place to more common and less brotherly modes of relief. A nest of small households enclosed, on three sides, an open space devoted to gardens, in which each had a share. Here each poor family lived in separate rooms, and were assisted by the Society, according to its needs.... These paupers were oftentimes ministers and elders,.... Everything conspired to make them retain undiminished self-respect." (*LNY*, 194) While writing the "Letters from New York," Child lived with Isaac T. Hopper's Quaker family and was undoubtedly influenced by the family's extensive involvement in reforms, including antislavery and prison reform. She wrote admiringly of both Isaac and his daughter, Abby Hopper Gibbons. By 1845, Abby and several other women formed the Female Department of the New York Prison Association, which, later that year, opened the first halfway house in the world designed to help a large number of female prisoners find employment and housing after their release from prison. See

Margaret Hope Bacon, *Abby Hopper Gibbons: Prison Reformer and Social Activist*, 54.

19. For more on Child's fear that Andrew Johnson's administration was undercutting the promises of emancipation and for more on her primer, *The Freedmen's Book*, see Karcher, *The First Woman in the Republic: A Cultural Biography of Lydia Maria Child*, 487–531.

20. Child's responses to middle-class and working-class children are characteristic of what Jacques Donzelot describes as the modern disciplinary apparatus focused on children. Analyzing developments in France, Donzelot theorizes that the relationship between the state and the family and the very nature of the family underwent a dramatic transformation with the rise of industrial capitalism and the disciplinary apparatuses Child supported. He theorizes that two different family structures emerged from this transformation. On the one hand, medical doctors and advice writers collaborated with the middle-class mother, enhancing the importance of her social role. On the other hand, a burgeoning structure of educators, social workers, and truancy court officers converged on working-class children, often severely limiting the authority of working-class parents. While this social complex provided the bourgeois family with a "protected liberation" in which individual members were shielded from the arbitrary will of the head of the family and children from the "dangers" of servants' influence, the working-class family was subjected to more intense scrutiny and limitation. The working-class's contact with the social resulted in "supervised freedom," a system of tutelage imposed from without, rather than through mothers leagued with a socializing apparatus. See Donzelot, *The Policing of Families*, 18–22 and 45–7.

21. While Olmsted sprinkled his surveys of the South with references to the South's underdeveloped civil society, he elaborated on the significance of social institutions on pages 554–9 in *The Cotton Kingdom*.

22. See Donzelot, *The Policing of Families*, and Lasch, *Haven in a Heartless World*. As Kathryn Kish Sklar reminds us, "welfare state" is an anachronistic term rejected by labor and working-class leaders for its condescending connotation of need rather than right; see "The Historical Foundations of Women's Power in the Creation of the American Welfare State, 1830–1930," 48–9.

CHAPTER 3

1. See "*The Scarlet Letter* and Revolutions Abroad" in Larry Reynolds' *European Revolutions and the American Literary Renaissance*. Reynolds argues that the conservatives revived imagery from the French Revolution of 1789 to describe the events of 1848–1849 in Europe. These images, appearing in Democratic Party papers and used to describe President Zachary Taylor's firing of political appointees, influenced Hawthorne's own imagery in "The Custom House" and *The Scarlet Letter*. In addition, Hawthorne was reading Alphonse de Lamartine's *History of the Girondists*, a history sympathetic to

the royal family during the French Revolution, at the very time that he began writing *The Scarlet Letter* (88).

2. David Brion Davis argues that many historians of slavery have exaggerated the guilt that defenders of slavery felt over the apparent contradiction between their ideals of liberty and democracy and their reality of slavery. Davis countered that many Americans had accommodated their moral code so that it muted any perceptible conflict between ideals and actions. For example, even today, many readers accept Daniel Defoe's Robinson Crusoe as a model of self-sufficiency, forgetting that Crusoe was a Brazilian planter and slaveowner prior to his adventure on the island. By repressing certain elements in a narrative, Americans could reconcile their ideals to their actions. See David Brion Davis, "Slavery and the American Mind."

3. See Jennifer Fleischner, "Hawthorne and the Politics of Slavery," and Jean Fagan Yellin, "Hawthorne and the American National Sin," for a complete rehearsal of the limited references to slavery in Hawthorne's notebooks, letters, and campaign biography of Franklin Pierce.

4. "Old News" was originally published in 1835 in the *New England Magazine* and republished in *The Snow Image* (1851). It is premised on old newspapers dating back to the 1690s.

5. Ellen Meiksins Wood distinguishes between "societies with markets and trade, which have existed throughout recorded history, and the specificity of capitalism, where 'the market' is not an opportunity but an imperative" (289). Once western farmers began underselling smaller, less fertile New England farms and industrial production moved out of the household to more centralized factories in the United States, the market became an imperative for most Americans. Stephanie Coontz locates this transformation between 1815–1855. See Ellen Meiksins Wood, *Democracy against Capitalism*, and Coontz, *The Social Origins of Private Life*.

6. John Jentz discovers that the class composition of antislavery activists evolves throughout the Jacksonian period as upper-class patrons give way to more working-class advocates. See John Jentz, "The Antislavery Constituency in Jacksonian New York City."

7. Child's post–Civil War novel, *Romance of the Republic*, represents an extension of the Garrisonian abolitionists' vision of a national family. While the Garrisonians were successful in destroying the image of paternalistic slaveholders among Northerners in the 1850s, following the Civil War, images of fratricidal (white) conflict replaced images of the slavemart as the primary threat to the nation. Child's novel was an unusual post–Civil War vision of national unification brought about through interracial marriage and adoption. More common visions include the racist novels of Thomas Dixon, culminating in D.W. Griffiths's adaptation of a Dixon novel, "Birth of a Nation." The new national metaphor became that of white "brothers" North and South reconciling by marrying one another's sisters and defeating African American political and social aspirations.

8. Raymond Williams uses the phrase "economic limits and pressures" to describe the relationship between economic forces and cultural phenomena,

including political discourse. Williams rejects a model of economic determinism in which cultural forms are the inevitable by-product of the economic base. He also rejects a Foucauldian model of discourse in which economic forces have little or no influence on the popular validity of various truth claims. See Raymond Williams, *Problems in Materialism and Culture*, especially 31–32.

9. See Jim O'Loughlin, "Articulating Uncle Tom's Cabin." O'Loughlin writes, "the cultural power of Stowe's novel came from its connection of existing tropes and public concerns in a compelling narrative form" (593). Stowe successfully rearticulated popular cultural elements, putting them in the service of the antislavery cause, a strategy at which antislavery writers became especially adept.

10. See Philip Lapsansky, "Graphic Discord: Abolitionist and Anti-abolitionist Images," for a comparison between the visual campaigns of abolitionists and anti-abolitionists. He argues the anti-abolitionists "carried the day" following the Civil War with their "clichéd dandified, malapropic blacks, grotesque black women, and white reforming harridans" (230).

11. Following the publication of Harriet Beecher Stowe's *Uncle Tom's Cabin*, there was a spate of anti-Uncle Tom novels, including Mary Eastman's *Aunt Phillis's Cabin* and J. Thornton Randolph's *The Cabin and Parlor*. These too can be seen as rearticulations of antislavery signs, specifically the sign of the slave cabin. If the cabin represents the fragility of the black family under slavery, these anti-Uncle Tom novels suggest the best guarantor of the slave family's stability, following George Fitzhugh's logic, is the benevolent master. Such defenses were unusual, however, and proslavery forces more commonly circulated defenses in political-economic treatises like Thomas Dew's or political speeches like John C. Calhoun's.

12. See Leland Person, "The Dark Labyrinth of Mind: Hawthorne, Hester and the Ironies of Racial Mothering."

13. To account for changes in the ways in which people feel and understand their experience, Raymond Williams uses the phrase "structures of feeling." The phrase emphasizes the personal and present nature of social experience that is not wholly determined by changes in "institutions, formations, and beliefs" nor by "changing social and economic relationships" (131). Structures of feeling "do not have to await definition, classification, or rationalization before they exert palpable pressures and set effective limits on experience and on action" (132). See Raymond Williams, *Marxism and Literature*. Williams recognizes the difference between meanings and values actively felt and beliefs formally acknowledged. While Hawthorne was more anti-abolitionist than antislavery, an abhorrence for and obsession with antislavery depictions of the slave mother structured his feelings toward labor, gender relations, and the domestic sphere.

14. One indication of Nathaniel and Sophia Hawthorne's suspicion of public, governmental incursions into the family came with their decision to educate their children at home. Sophia's sister Elizabeth Peabody had long taught at private schools and run her own private school. Sophia's other sister, Mary,

married Horace Mann, champion of the public school movement and the first secretary of the Massachusetts Board of Education (1837–1848). Mann resigned from the board when he was elected to the U.S. House of Representatives as an antislavery Whig. On the issues of slavery and public education, both "family issues," Mann's vision of government intervention was directly at odds with Hawthorne's more conservative, Democratic vision. See T. Walter Herbert's family biography of the Hawthornes, *Dearest Beloved: The Hawthornes and the Makings of the Middle-Class Family*, for an elaboration of the influence of middle-class ideology on relations between Nathaniel and Sophia Hawthorne and between the Hawthornes and their children.

15. For a detailed description of the products produced primarily by women and meant to induce antislavery loyalties, see Michael Bennett's vivid "tour" of the National Anti-Slavery Bazaar in Chapter 1 of *Democratic Discourses: The Radical Abolition Movement and Antebellum American Literature*.

16. Fanny Fern and Susan Warner are just two examples of popular women authors who wrote under extreme financial pressure. Fern, an author Hawthorne admired, wrote explicitly about this pressure in *Ruth Hall*.

17. See Michel de Certeau, *The Practice of Everyday Life*.

18. Hawthorne's subsequent portrait of Zenobia and Hollingsworth in *The Blithedale Romance* makes just this point. In *The Blithedale Romance*, Hollingsworth pursues prison reform as a means of enhancing his own self-importance. Zenobia adopts his scheme to win Hollingsworth and makes dramatic speeches about women's rights as a means of drawing attention to herself. Self-interest taints their motives. Ambition leads Hollingsworth to court the wealthy Zenobia, leading to a fatal mix of domestic and commercial aspirations.

19. This scene stands in stark contrast to another one Hawthorne might have drawn, one based on a family scandal. His own mother's ancestors were similarly subject to public humiliation for sexual transgressions. In 1680, Anstiss and Margaret Manning were convicted of incest with their brother, who fled Salem. They were sentenced to sit on a high stool in the Salem meeting house wearing paper caps that read "incest." The picture of these two women, similarly forced to face public humiliation while their male partner escaped, is, nevertheless, a far more degrading picture. They sit rather than stand; they are not called upon to speak; they make no sign of resistance. Hawthorne' retelling of the scene in antislavery iconography has the effect of lending Hester much greater dignity. See Vernon Loggins, *The Hawthorne's: Seven Generations of an American Family*. 88–93.

CHAPTER 4

1. Twelve Southern writers published *I'll Take My Stand* in 1930 to protest the U.S. commitment to industrial capitalism and what they viewed as a materialistic and spiritually impoverished approach to life. They advocated a life close to the soil and traditional, hierarchical family and racial relations.

2. Lauren Berlant examines the operation of sentimentality and argues that it only temporarily permits women to break the prohibition against women speaking in the public sphere. "... [A]t moments of crisis persons violate the zones of privacy that give them privilege and protection in order to fix something social that feels threatening. They become public on behalf of privacy and imagine that their rupture of individuality by collective action is temporary and will be healed when the national world is once again safe for a return to personal life. Sentimental politics works on behalf of its own eradication" (647). See "Poor Eliza," 635–68.

3. See Jessica Benjamin, *Bonds of Love*, for a full theorization of female masochistic desire. Paradoxically, Mary can achieve the recognition she desires from her husband, who represents all of the outside world, only by utterly effacing herself. When she had directly approached him, he had rejected her as a "shrew," as a woman inappropriately adopting the prerogatives of masculinity. Benjamin explains that masochism "is a search for recognition through an other who is powerful enough to bestow this recognition. This other has the power for which the self longs, and through his recognition she gains it, though vicariously" (56). In Southworth's text, Mary's sister operates as a foil who is severely punished in the text for her aggressive behavior. See "The Married Shrew."

4. Southworth sets the book in 1844–45, a period during which Child penned some of her "Letters from New York." Given Southworth's connection to the antislavery press, it is quite likely she would have read Child's letters in their original context or in the reprinted book form and would have been familiar with her depiction of street urchins. Living in Washington, D.C., especially prior to 1850 when the slave trade was legal in the nation's capital, Southworth was likely less sensitive to the urban exploitation of children than she was to the effects of slaveholding patriarchy on white women and children. Further shutting off potential criticisms of wage labor was the critical juncture during which Southworth wrote, in 1859, as John Brown forced the nation's hand and, as Sacvan Bercovitch has argued, the possibility of sectional compromise receded into a discourse of "either/or," a national system of slave labor or wage labor. See Sacvan Bercovitch, *The Office of the Scarlet Letter*.

5. Southworth writes the novel in the early years of the Newsboys' Lodging Houses, established by the Children's Aid Society in New York City. These lodging houses were meant to offer free housing and food as well as a domesticating influence to "street arabs," children who were homeless and earning wages in the street. Karen Sanchez-Eppler analyzes the middle-class rhetoric on homeless boys and girls and finds that in Children's Aid Society reports the newsboy is a figure of working-class play; while aid workers lament the absence of softening influences on such boys, they depict the boys' work as a form of play, mitigating the sense that these boys are exploited. Homeless girls, on the other hand, are exclusively objects of pity or fear. Charles Loring Brace writes in one report, "With a boy 'Arab of the streets,' one always has the consolation that, despite his ragged clothes and bed in a box

or hay barge, he often has a rather good time of it, and enjoys many of the delicious pleasures of a child's roving life, and that a fortunate turn of events may at anytime make an honest, industrious, fellow of him . . . . With a girl vagrant it is different" (qtd. in Sanchez-Eppler 831–32).

6. E.D.E.N. Southworth, *Ishmael; or, in the Depths* and *The Curse of Clifton.*

7. Coverture is the legal doctrine, derived from English Common Law, that held that the woman was absorbed into (covered by) the legal identity of her husband by marriage. Her person, property, and wages became his, and he entered into contracts, paid taxes, or served on juries on her behalf. It governed women's legal standing in the United States until 1848 when New York passed the Married Women's Property Laws, which enhanced the rights and contractual powers of wives. Other states used New York as a model and enacted incremental reforms throughout the last half of the nineteenth century.

8. See Robert Jones, *The Hidden Hand, A Drama in Five Acts.* The role of Wool was played with great success by Frank S. Chanfrau when the play moved from the working-class Bowery to a middle-class Broadway venue (Odell, 317). Chanfrau was famous for playing Mose in *A Glance at New York*, an Irish Bowery b'hoy with a captivating, pugilistic working-class pride. He is credited (or blamed by some middle-class theater critics) with democratizing middle-class theaters when Chanfrau's National Theater permitted working-class patrons to sit anywhere in the theater rather than exclusively in the pit. Chanfrau was a working-class hero, and it is significant that he took on the role of Wool in this play about class mobility (Richardson, 277–78, and Buckley, 459–61). Wool himself becomes a more important and con-frontational character in the 1867 Robert Jones play. He takes on some of the characteristics of the Bowery b'hoy when he fights Craven Le Noir in the forced marriage scene.

9. One indication that this novel resists the ideology of true womanhood permeating Southworth's other works is that despite *The Hidden Hand*'s pop-ularity, she consistently claimed that another novel, a far more conventional melodrama, *Ishmael; or, In the Depths*, was her favorite (Boyle, 67).

10. *The Hidden Hand* first appeared on stage in 1858 at the working-class Bow-ery theater where Fanny Herring, an actress famous for her "breaches roles," played Capitola (Odell, 140). It then played in more middle-class venues including the National Theater, Barnum's Museum, and the Broadway Boudoir (Odell).

11. Capitola became such a beloved character that a California seaside town and race horses were named after her.

CHAPTER 5

1. Farley speculates that Brownson's prejudice against factory girls stemmed from the common assumption that factory operatives in New England

worked under conditions similar to those under which English factory operatives worked. In subsequent articles, Farley repeatedly cites the description
of English factory operatives in "The Factory System," a frequently quoted
1833 article from the English periodical *Blackwood's Edinburgh Magazine*.
Farley dwells upon the article's depiction of child labor, the "waste of infants."
For Farley, the English system deserved its comparison to slavery as children were "purchased from their parents at a low price" to be ground up
by machines ("Editorial: The Factory System,"). See also Farley, "Editorial:
Health."

2. Ava Baron argues that historians have looked for working-class resistance in
   union activism and strikes, to the exclusion of other forms of resistance that
   women more commonly use. The public relations campaign launched by
   the *Lowell Offering* was no less effective than the strikes of 1834 and 1836
   in pressuring the corporations to improve work conditions and compensation. Moreover, the *Lowell Offering*'s campaign was wider in scope than the
   strikes, targeting not only the mill owners but a larger American audience.
   The writers hoped that by demonstrating the intelligence and dignity of
   female factory operatives, public pressure would discourage the owners from
   allowing work conditions to deteriorate further. See Ava Baron, "Gender
   and Labor History," in *Work Engendered: Toward a New History of American
   Labor*.

3. See David Roediger, *Wages of Whiteness*, especially Chapter 4, "White Slaves,
   Wage Slaves and Free White Labor." Some male labor leaders described
   female factory workers as slaves while resisting the label for themselves.
   Like male labor leaders, women did not refer to themselves as wage slaves
   but deferred such a scenario into the future if wages and work conditions
   deteriorated further. At the 1836 strike, Lowell women sang,

   > Oh! I cannot be a slave;
   > I will not be a slave.
   > For I'm so fond of liberty
   > That I cannot be a slave. (69)

4. One writer rebuts the phrase "white slave of the north" with a detailed sum-
   mary of a factory woman's day. She writes, "Much has been said of the factory
   girl and her employment. By some she has been represented as dwelling in a
   sort of brick-and-mortar paradise . . . Others have deemed her a mere servile
   drudge, chained to her labor by almost as strong a power as that which holds
   a bondsman in his fetters; and, indeed, some have already given her the title
   of 'the white slave of the North.' Her real situation approaches neither one
   nor the other of these extremes" ("A Week in the Mills" 217).

5. Concurrent with the *Lowell Offering*'s publication, William Lloyd Garrison, editor of the antislavery newspaper *The Liberator*, wrote many articles
   supporting Irish tenant farmers against English landlords and supporting
   English Chartists. Gerrit Smith wrote in the pages of the *Working Man's*

Advocate that, while the slave's oppression was far worse than that of the wage laborer, the two groups shared much in common. His experiment of selling land in Elba, NY, on easy terms to former slaves was aimed at helping them to establish independence as Brownson defined it. Douglass compared white shipyard workers in Baltimore to slaves who mistakenly viewed their black counterparts as threats. According to Douglass, the white workers failed to see that the slaveowners and capitalists played one group off the other to keep wages low.

6. Herbert Shapiro finds evidence that hundreds of Lowell's factory women were members of the antislavery society there and signed antislavery petitions. Philip Foner adds that the Lowell Female Labor Reform Association, founded in January 1845, officially participated in antislavery meetings and circulated antislavery petitions. See Foner, *Women and the American Labor Movement*, and Shapiro, "Labor and Antislavery: Reflections on the Literature."

7. In her study of "woman's fiction" dominating American literature between 1820 and 1870, Nina Baym finds "scarcely any . . . novels of seduction" (26). Domestic ideology rejected the figure of the woman dominated by her emotions, the "inevitable sexual prey." Sentimental heroines transcended their sexuality rather than falling victim to it. Michael Denning argues that the seduction story returns after 1870 with the important difference that it became a means of discussing class oppression. The seducer/rapist was of a higher class than the working girl, and the working girl usually just escaped his persecution. Neither notes the persistence of the seduction narrative in antislavery fiction that acts as a bridge to the class inflections Denning discovers in the later seduction tales. See Baym, *Woman's Fiction: A Guide to Novels by and about Women in America, 1820–1870*, and Denning, *Mechanic Accents: Dime Novels and Working-Class Culture in America*.

8. In an interesting conjunction, Lydia Maria Child used the metaphor of a broom brought to life to describe women's political awakening. Clergymen who urged women to become missionaries and form tract societies changed "a household utensil to a living energetic being and they have no spell to turn it into a broom again." See Carolyn Karcher, *The First Woman in the Republic: A Cultural Biography of Lydia Maria Child* 322.

9. According to Carl Siracusa, Massachusetts was the most industrialized area outside of England by 1860. See *A Mechanical People: Perceptions of the Industrial Order in Massachusetts, 1815–1850* 16–39.

10. See Sean Wilentz, *Chants Democratic* 335–43.

11. Ibid. 341.

12. David Roediger in *Wages of Whiteness* says that the term "white slavery" was used far more frequently than "slavery of wages" or "wage slavery" before the Civil War, in part because the term did not challenge the enslavement of blacks in the South. He writes,

> Moreover, it should be obvious that for all but a handful of committed abolitionists/labor reformers, use of a term like *white slavery* was not

an act of solidarity with the slave but rather a call to arms to end the inappropriate oppression of whites. Critiques of white slavery took form, after all, alongside race riots, racially exclusive trade unions, continuing use of terms like *boss* and *help* to deny comparison with slaves, the rise of minstrel shows, and popular campaigns to attack further the meager civil rights of free Blacks. (68–9)

13. By 1846, however, one article made an extensive comparison between wagons bringing girls to the factories and slave ships, concluding, "Philanthropists may talk of Negro slavery, but it would be well first to endeavor to emancipate the slaves at home. Let us not stretch our ears to catch the sound of the lash on the flesh of the oppressed black while the oppressed in our very midst are crying out in thunder tones, and calling upon us for assistance" ("Recruitment of Female Operatives").

14. See, for example, the denunciation of William Schouler, editor of the *Lowell Courier* and former publisher of the *Lowell Offering*, for not supporting the Lowell petition for a ten-hour workday. Calling him "the tool sent by the Lowell Corporations to the Massachusetts Legislator," the editors led an attack on Schouler that culminated in his failure to be reelected to the legislature ("An Operative").

15. See Ann Douglas, *The Feminization of American Culture* 70–71.

16. See Viola 52–3. In antislavery feminist terms, the narrator pleads with women, "And need we the eloquence of man to enlist our charity in the cause of a wronged and suffering sister?" (53).

CHAPTER 6

1. See John Stauffer's *Black Hearts of Men* 158–59.

2. Elizabeth Cady Stanton and Susan B. Anthony discovered their gift for organizing and agitating within the antislavery movement, but after the Civil War the American Equal Rights Association split when it became clear that legislation enfranchising both women and black men would not pass Congress. When former abolitionists claimed it was the "Negro's hour" and recommended dropping demands for women's voting rights, Stanton and Anthony bolted from the organization. Anthony made invidious distinctions between the intelligence of African American men and that of white women, insisting that black men should not get the vote before women. William Lloyd Garrison, Wendell Phillips, and Gerritt Smith, men who were now well past their prime and anxious to be able to declare victory and rest, considered their work done after passage of the Fourteenth and Fifteenth Amendments. Phillips disbanded the American Anti-Slavery Society, and Garrison ceased publishing the *Liberator*. See McFeely, *All on Fire* 265–69, and Mayer, *Frederick Douglass*, 597–614.

3. In Sumner's "Crime against Kansas," he accuses Southerners of raping Kansas, making them even more brutal than Turks, popularly associated with misogyny and oppression: "It is the rape of a virgin Territory, compelling it

to the hateful embrace of Slavery; and it may be clearly traced to a depraved longing for a new slave State, the hideous offspring of such a crime, in the hope of adding to the power of slavery in the National Government. Yes, sir, when the whole world, alike Christian and Turk, is rising up to condemn this wrong, and to make it a hissing to the nations, here in our Republic, force, ay, sir, FORCE has been openly employed in compelling Kansas to this pollution, and all for the sake of political power."

4. Lydia Maria Child, referring to the Tartars of the Central Asian region near Russia and Turkey, claimed that the "ceremony of marriage consists in placing the bride on a mat, and consigning her to the bridegroom, with the words, 'Here, wolf, take thy lamb'" ("Letters from New York, No. 34" 360).

5. See David W. Blight's seminal work, *Frederick Douglass' Civil War: Keeping Faith in Jubilee*, especially Chapter 7, "Douglass and the Meaning of the Black Soldier," and Chapter 10, "Douglass and the Struggle for the Memory of the Civil War."

6. In antislavery literature, the African diaspora was frequently represented as a woman appealing to God (and the reader) through Christ-like imagery. The image drew upon Psalm 68:31, "Princes shall come out of Egypt; Ethiopia shall soon stretch out her hands unto God." Frances Ellen Watkins Harper's poem "Ethiopia" is a good example of how antislavery writers adapted the trope: "Yes! Ethiopia yet shall stretch/ Her bleeding hands abroad; / Her cry of agony shall reach/ The burning throat of God." Douglass himself published the poem in *Frederick Douglass' Paper* on March 31, 1854, at the height of his antislavery agitation.

7. In 1892, Ida B. Wells printed an article defending three of her friends who had been lynched. While defending their store from armed white competitors who, jealous of the men's success in the grocery business, had killed the men to eliminate competition. Under personal threat, she left town, and her paper, the *Memphis Free Press*, was destroyed. Alexander Manly's press was destroyed in 1898 as the culmination of a hysterical response to his editorial in which he argued that poor white women had consensual affairs with black men. When the affairs became public, he argued, the black men were accused of rape and lynched to protect the honor of the white woman. See Wells, *On Lynchings: Southern Horrors, A Red Record, Mob Rule in New Orleans*; and Eric Sundquist's "Introduction" to *The Marrow of Tradition* by Charles Chesnutt.

8. See also Frederick Douglass, "Vote the Regular Republican Ticket: An Address Delivered in Raleigh, North Carolina on July 25, 1872."

9. Douglass would undoubtedly have been more pleased by the African American Civil War Memorial sculpted by Ed Hamilton in 1997 and erected in the capital. The front of the statue reveals four black soldiers (three infantry and one sailor), and the back depicts a young black man leaving his family for war.

WORKS CITED

Abate, Michele Ann. "Launching a Gender B(l)acklash: E.D.E.N. Southworth's The Hidden Hand and the Emergence of (Racialized) White Tomboyism." *Children's Literature Association Quarterly.* 31.1(2006): 40–64. Project Muse. Web. 15 June 2007.

Addams, Jane. *Twenty Years at Hull House, with Autobiographical Notes.* 1910. New York: Signet Classic, 1938. Print.

A.F.D. "Life Among the Farmers." *Lowell Offering.* Vol. 2. Lowell: Powers and Bagley, 1842. 129–37. Print.

A Factory Girl [Harriet Farley]. "Factory Girls." *Lowell Offering.* Dec. 1840: 17–18. Print.

A.G.A. "Editorial." *Lowell Offering.* Vol. 4. Lowell: Misses Curtis and Farley, 1844. Print.

Altschuler, Glenn C. and Stuart M. Blumin. "'Where is the Real America?': Politics and Popular Consciousness in the Antebellum Era." *American Quarterly* 49.2 (June 1997): 225–67. Print.

Alvez, Susan. "'My Sisters Toil': Voice in Anti-Slavery Poetry by White Female Factory Workers." *Multiculturalism: Roots and Realities.* Ed. C. James Trotman. Bloomington: Indiana UP, 2002. 139–54. Print.

The Amistad Case. 1840. New York: Johnson Reprint Corporation, 1968. Print.

Anbinder, Tyler. "We Will Dirk Every Mother's Son of You": Five Points and the Irish Conquest of New York Politics," *Eire-Ireland: A Journal of Irish Studies* 29 (Spring-Summer 2001): 29–46. Print.

Andrews, William L. *Critical Essays on Frederick Douglass.* Boston: G.K. Hall & Co., 1991. Print.

"Anniversary Week." *Voice of Industry.* 12 June 1845: 2. Print.

Ashworth, John. *Slavery, Capitalism, and Politics in the Antebellum Republic.* Vol. 1. Cambridge: Cambridge UP, 1995. Print.

———. "The Relationship between Capitalism and Humanitarianism." *American Historical Review* 92.4 (Oct. 1987): 813–28. Print.

Bacon, Margaret Hope. *Abby Hopper Gibbons: Prison Reformer and Social Activist.* Albany: SUNY Press, 2000. Print.

Baron, Ava. "Gender and Labor History." *Work Engendered: Toward a New History of American Labor.* Ed. Ava Baron. Ithaca: Cornell UP, 1991. Print.

Baym, Nina. *American Women Writers and the Work of History, 1790–1860.* New Brunswick, Rutgers UP, 1995. Print.

——. *Woman's Fiction: A Guide to Novels by and about Women in America, 1820–1870*. Ithaca: Cornell UP, 1978. Print.

Benjamin, Jessica. *The Bonds of Love: Psychoanalysis, Feminism, and the Problem of Domination*. New York: Pantheon Books, 1988. Print.

Bennett, Michael. *Democratic Discourses: The Radical Abolition Movement and Antebellum American Literature*. New Brunswick: Rutgers UP, 2005. Print.

Bentley, Nancy. "The Mulatta Hero in Antebellum Fiction." *Subjects and Citizens: Nation, Race, and Gender from Oroonoko to Anita Hill*. Durham: Duke UP, 1995. 195–216. Print.

Bercovitch, Sacvan. *The Office of the Scarlet Letter*. Baltimore: Johns Hopkins UP, 1991. Print.

Berlant, Lauren. "Poor Eliza." *American Literature* 70.3 (September 1998): 635–68. Print.

"A Big Grant and Wilson Meeting." *Richmond Daily Dispatch* 24 July 1872: 1. Print.

Blight, David W. *Frederick Douglass' Civil War: Keeping Faith in Jubilee*. Baton Rouge: Louisiana State UP, 1989. Print.

Boyle, Regis Louise. *Mrs. E.D.E.N. Southworth, Novelist*. Washington D.C.: Catholic University Press, 1939. Print.

Brown, Gillian. *Domestic Individualism: Imagining Self in Nineteenth-Century America*. Berkeley: University of California Press, 1990. Print.

Brownson, Orestes. "The Laboring Classes." *The Boston Quarterly Review* 3.11 (July 1840): 358–95. Print.

Buckley, Peter G. "Paratheatricals and Popular Stage Entertainment." *The Cambridge History of American Theater*. Ed. Don B. Wilmeth and Christopher Bigsby. New York: Cambridge UP, 1998. 424–81. Print.

Calhoun. John C. *The Essential Calhoun*. Ed. Clyde N. Wilson. New Brunswick: Transactions Publishers, 1992. Print.

Certeau, Michel de. *The Practice of Everyday Life*. Trans. Steven Rendall.Berkeley: University of California Press, 1984. Print.

Child, Lydia Maria. *An Appeal in Favor of Americans Called Africans*. 1836. New York: Arno Press, 1968. Print.

——. *Anti-Slavery Catechism*. 2nd ed. Newburyport, MA: Charles Whipple, 1835. *Internet Archive*. Web. 15 May 2009.

——. "The Cottage Girl." *The Juvenile Miscellany* September 1828: 3–19. Print.

——. *The Freedmen's Book*. 1865. New York: Arno Press, 1968. Print.

——. *Letters from New York*. New York: Charles S. Francis and Co., 1843. Print.

——. "Letters from New York, No. 34." 1843. Rpt. in *A Lydia Maria Child Reader*. 358–64. Print.

——. "Louisa Preston." *The Juvenile Miscellany* March 1828: 56–81. Print.

——. *A Lydia Maria Child Reader*. Ed. Carolyn Karcher. Durham: Duke UP, 1997. Print.

——. *Lydia Maria Child Selected Letters, 1817–1880*. Ed. Milton Meltzer and Patricia G. Holland. Assoc. Ed. Francine Krasno. Amherst: University of Massachusetts Press, 1982. Print.

——. "The Quadroons." *The Liberty Bell*. Boston: Massachusetts Anti-Slavery Fair, 1842. 115–41. Print.

——. "Reply of Mrs. Child." *Correspondence between Lydia Maria Child and Gov. Wise and Mrs. Mason of Virginia*. 1859. Rpt. in *A Lydia Maria Child Reader*. 243–53. Print.

——. *A Romance of the Republic*. 1867. New York: Book Jungle, 2007. Print.

——. "Rosy O'Ryan." *A New Flower for Children*. New York: C.S. Francis & Co. 1856. 158–87. Print.

——. "Slavery's Pleasant Homes." *The Liberty Bell* 1843: 147–60. Rpt. in *A Lydia Maria Child Reader*. 238–42. Print.

——. "Uncollected Letter." *Boston Courier* 6 February 1844. Rpt. in *A Lydia Maria Child Reader*. 365–373. Print.

——. "Women's Rights: Letters from New York, No. 50." 1843. Rpt. in *The Heath Anthology*. 2nd ed. Vol. 1. Ed. Paul Lauter et al. Lexington, MA: D.C. Heath and Co., 1994. 1837–1840. Print.

Coontz, Stephanie. *The Social Origins of Private Life: A History of American Families 1600–1900*. New York: Verso, 1988. Print.

Cott, Nancy F. "Young Women in the Second Great Awakening in New England." *Feminist Studies* 2 (1975): 15–29. Print.

Cronin, Morton. "Hawthorne on Romantic Love and the Status of Women." *PMLA* 69.1 (March 1954): 89–98. *JSTOR*. Web. 30 May 2007.

"Cruelties of Slavery." *The Anti-Slavery Record* 1.5 (May 1835): 49. Print.

D. [Eliza J. Kate] "Leisure Hours of the Mill Girls." *Lowell Offering* Vol. 2. Lowell: Powers and Bagley, 1842. 65–79. Print.

Dall, Caroline W. Healey. "Pictures of Southern Life, for the Drawing Rooms of American Women." *The Liberty Bell*. Boston: Massachusetts Anti-Slavery Fair, 1851. Print.

Davis, David Brion. *The Problem of Slavery in Wester Culture*. Ithaca: Cornell UP, 1966. Print.

——. "Reflections on Abolitionism and Ideological Hegemony." *American Historical Review* 92.4 (Oct. 1987): 797–812. Print.

——. "Slavery and the American Mind." *Perspectives and Irony in American Slavery*. Ed. by Harry Owens. Jackson, Miss.: Mississippi UP, 1976. Print.

Denning, Michael. *Mechanic Accents: Dime Novels and Working-Class Culture in America*. New York: Verso, 1987. Print.

"The Desperation of a Mother." *The Anti-Slavery Record* 1.9 (September 1835): 101. Print.

Deyle, Steven. *Carry Me Back: The Domestic Slave Trade in American Life*. New York: Oxford UP, 2005. Print.

Diner, Steven J. *A Very Different Age: Americans of the Progressive Era*. New York: Hill and Wang, 1998. Print.

Dobson, Joanne and Amy E. Hudock. "E.D.E.N. Southworth." *Dictionary of Literary Biography*. Vol. 239: American Women Prose Writers, 1820–1870. Ed. Amy E. Hudock and Katharine Rodier. Detroit: The Gale Group, 2001. Print.

Dobson, Joanne. "The Hidden Hand: Subversion of Cultural Ideology in Three Mid-Nineteenth-Century American Women's Novels." *American Quarterly* 38.2 (Summer 1986): 223–42. JSTOR. Web. 1 June 2007.

Dobson, Joanne. Introduction. *The Hidden Hand; or, Capitola the Madcap.* By E.D.E.N. Southworth. New Brunswick, NJ: Rutgers UP, 1988. Print.

Donzelot, Jacques. *The Policing of Families.* Trans. Robert Hurley. New York: Pantheon Books, 1979. Print.

Douglas, Ann. The Feminization of American Culture. New York: Doubleday, 1977. Print.

Douglass, Frederick. "Cheap Labor." 1871. *Life and Writings of Frederick Douglass.* Vol. 4. 264–66. Print.

——. "The Color Question: An Address Delivered in Washington, D.C. on July 5, 1875." *The Frederick Douglass Papers.* Series 1, Vol. 4. 414–22. Print.

——. *The Frederick Douglass Papers.* Series 1: Speeches, Debates, and Interviews, Vol. 3: 1855–1863. Ed. John W. Blassingame. New Haven, Yale UP, 1985. Print.

——. *The Frederick Douglass Papers.* Series 1: Speeches, Debates, and Interviews, Vol. 4: 1864–1880. Ed. John W. Blassingame and John R. McKivigan. New Haven, Yale UP, 1991. Print.

——. "The Freedman's Monument to Abraham Lincoln: An Address Delivered in Washington, D.C. on March 13, 1876." *The Frederick Douglass Papers.* Series 1, Vol. 4. 427–40. Print.

——. "An Inside View of Slavery: An Address Delivered in Boston, Massachusetts on February 8, 1855." *The Frederick Douglass Papers.* Series 1, Vol. 3. 5–14. Print.

——. "The Labor Question." 1871. *Life and Writings of Frederick Douglass.* Vol. 4. 282–85. Print.

——. "Let the Negro Alone: An Address Delivered in New York, NY on May 11, 1869." *The Frederick Douglass Papers.* Series 1, Vol. 4. 199–213. Print.

——. "Let the Negro Alone." *The New York Herald* 12 May 1869: 3. Print.

——. *The Life and Writings of Frederick Douglass.* Vol. 4: Reconstruction and After. Ed. Philip S. Foner. New York: International Publishers, 1955. Print.

——. *My Bondage and My Freedom.* Ed. William L. Andrews. Urbana: University of Illinois Press, 1987. Print.

——. *Narrative of the Life of Frederick Douglass.* 1845. New York: Signet Classic, 1968. Print.

——. "New Hampshire for the Republicans: An Address Delivered in Concord, NH on February 26, 1875." *The Frederick Douglass Papers.* Series 1, Vol. 401–07. Print.

——. "New Hampshire For the Republicans." *Concord Daily Monitor* 27 February 1875: 2. Print.

——. "The New Party Movement." *The Life and Writings of Frederick Douglass.* 254–57. Print.

——. "Our National Capital: An Address Delivered in Baltimore, MD on May 8, 1877." *The Frederick Douglass Papers.* Series 1, Vol. 4. 443–75. Print.

——. "Recollections of the Anti-Slavery Conflict: An Address Delivered in Louisville, KY on April 21, 1873." *The Frederick Douglass Papers*. Series 1, Vol. 4. 360–75.

——. "Salutatory of the Corresponding Editor." *The Life and Writings of Frederick Douglass*. 220–22. Print.

——. "The Unknown Dead: An Address Delivered in Arlington, VA on May 30, 1871." *The Frederick Douglass Papers*. Series 1, Vol. 4. 289–92. Print.

——. "Vote the Regular Republican Ticket: An Address Delivered in Raleigh, North Carolina on July 25, 1872." *The Frederick Douglass Papers*, Series 1, Vol. 4. 313–22. Print.

——. "We Are Here and Want the Ballot-Box: An Address Delivered in Philadelphia, PA on September 4, 1866." *The Frederick Douglass Papers*. Series 1, Vol. 4. 123–34. Print.

——. "We Are Here and Want the Ballot-Box." *The New York Herald* 5 September 1866: 3. Print.

——. "We Are Not Yet Quite Free: An Address Delivered in Medina, NY on August 3, 1869." *The Frederick Douglass Papers*. Series 1, Vol. 4. 220–40. Print.

——. "We Welcome the Fifteenth Amendment: An Address Delivered in New York, NY on May 12–13, 1869." *The Frederick Douglass Papers*. Series 1, Vol. 4. 213–20. Print.

——. "Which Greeley Are We Voting For?: An Address Delivered in Richmond, VA on July 24, 1872." *The Frederick Douglass Papers*. Series 1, Vol. 4. 302–13. Print.

Drescher, Seymour. *Econocide: British Slavery in the Era of Abolition*. Pittsburgh: University of Pittsburgh Press, 1977. Print.

Dublin, Thomas. *Farm to Factory: Women's Letters 1830–1860*. New York: Columbia University Press, 1981. Print.

DuBois, Ellen. "Women's Rights and Abolition: The Nature of the Connection." *Anti-Slavery Reconsidered: New Perspectives of the Abolitionists*. Ed. Lewis Perry and Michael Fellman. Baton Rouge: Louisiana State University Press, 1979. Print.

"The Duty of Wives." *Voice of Industry* 14 August 1845: 3. Print.

Ella [Harriet Farley]. "Conclusion of the Vol." *Lowell Offering* Vol. 1. Lowell: Powers and Bagley, 1841. 375–78. Print.

Eltis, David. *Economic Growth and the Ending of the Transatlantic Slave Trade*. New York: Oxford University Press, 1987. Print.

Ethelinda, "Prejudice Against Labor." *Lowell Offering* Vol. 1. Lowell: Powers and Bagley, 1841. 136–45. Print.

Evans, George Henry and John Windt. "The People's Cause." *The Working Man's Advocate* 24 May 1844: 2. Print.

——. "To Gerrit Smith." *The Working Man's Advocate* 6 July 1844: 3. Print.

——. "To the Public." *The Working Man's Advocate* 16 March 1844: 1. Print.

"Factory Labor." *Lowell Offering* Vol. 4. Lowell: Misses Curtis and Farley, 1844. 190–92. Print.

Farley, Harriet. "Editorial: Health." *Lowell Offering* Vol. 3. Lowell: William Schouler, 1843. 190–92. Print.

——. "Editorial: The Factory System." *Lowell Offering* Vol. 4. Lowell: Misses Curtis and Farley, 1844. 260. Print.

——. "Editorial: Two Suicides." *Lowell Offering* Vol. 4. Lowell: Misses Curtis and Farley, 1844. 212–15. Print.

Fitzhugh, George. "Southern Thought." *Heath Anthology of American Literature.* Vol. 1. 3rd ed. Ed. Paul Lauter. Boston: Houghton Mifflin Co., 1998. 2002–11. Print.

Fleischner, Jennifer. "Hawthorne and the Politics of Slavery." *Studies in the Novel* 23.1 (Spring 1991): 96–106. Print.

Foner, Eric. "Abolitionism and the Labor Movement in Ante-bellum America." *Politics and Ideology in the Age of the Civil War.* Ed. Eric Foner. New York: Oxford UP, 1980. 57–76. Print.

Foner, Philip. *Women and the American Labor Movement.* New York: The Free Press, 1979. Print.

Foucault, Michel. *Discipline and Punish: The Birth of the Prison.* Trans. Alan Sheridan. New York: Vintage Books, 1979. Print.

Frederickson, George M. "Uncle Tom and the Anglo Saxons: Romantic Racialism in the North." *The Black Image in the White Mind.* New York: Harper Collins, 1971. Rpt. in *Uncle Tom's Cabin.* Ed. Elizabeth Ammons. New York: Norton, 1994. 429–38. Print.

Ganter, Granville. " 'He Made Us Laugh Some': Frederick Douglass's Humor." *African American Review* 37.4 (Winter 2003): 535–52. *EBSCO Host.* Web. 28 May 2009.

Genovese, Eugene. *The Southern Front: History and Politics in the Cultural War.* Columbia: University of Missouri Press, 1995. Print.

Gramsci, Antonio. *Selections from the Prison Notebooks.* Eds. Quintin Hoare and Geoffrey Nowell Smith. New York: International Publishers, 1971. Print.

Grace [Harriot Curtis]. "Woman's Influence." *Lowell Offering* Vol. 3. Lowell: William Schouler, 1843. 218–25. Print.

Grimke, Angelina. "Appeal to the Christian Women of the South." *The Public Years of Sarah and Angelina Grimke.* Ed. Larry Ceplair. New York: Columbia University Press, 1989, 36–79. Print.

——. "Testimony of Angelina Grimke Weld." *The Public Years of Sarah and Angelina Grimke.* Ed. Larry Ceplair. New York: Columbia University Press, 1989. Print.

Gutman, Herbert, Ed. *Who Built America? Working People & the Nation's Economy, Politics, Culture & Society.* Vol. 1. New York: Pantheon Books, 1989. Print.

Habegger, Alfred. "A Well Hidden Hand." *Novel* 14 (1981): 197–212. Print.

Hannah. "History of a Hemlock Broom: Written By Itself." *Lowell Offering* Oct. 1840: 1–2. Print.

Harper, Frances Ellen Watkins. "Ethiopia." *The Norton Anthology of African American Literature.* 2nd ed. Ed. Henry Louis Gates Jr. and Nellie Y. McKay. New York: Norton, 2004. 494. Print.

Haskell, Thomas L. "Convention and Hegemonic Interest in the Debate Over Antislavery: A Reply to Davis and Ashworth." *American Historical Review* 92.4 (Oct. 1987): 829–78. Print.

Hawthorne, Nathaniel. *The American Notebooks.* New Haven: Yale UP, 1932. Print.

——. "The Custom House." *The Scarlet Letter.* New York: Scholastic Book Services, 1961. Print.

——. "Mrs Hutchinson." *The Heath Anthology of American Literature.* Vol. 1. Ed. Paul Lauter. Lexington: D.C. Heath and Co., 1994. 2315–19.

——. *The Scarlet Letter.* New York: Scholastic Book Services, 1961.

——. "Old News." *The Snow Image and Other Twice-Told Tales.* Boston: Fields, Osgood, and Co., 1869.

Hedrick, Joan D. *Harriet Beecher Stowe, a Life.* New York: Oxford UP, 1994. Print.

Hempstead, Martha. "The Fugitive." *The Liberty Bell.* Boston: Massachusetts Anti-Slavery Fair, 1845. Print.

Herbert, T. Walter. *Dearest Beloved: The Hawthornes and the Making of the Middle-Class Family.* Berkeley: University of California Press, 1993. Print.

Howard, June. *Form and History in American Literary Naturalism.* Chapel Hill: Univ. of North Carolina Press, 1985. Print.

Hudock, Amy E. "Challenging the Definition of Heroism in E.D.E. N. Southworth's *The Hidden Hand.*" *American Transcendental Quarterly* 9.1 (March 1995): 5–20. Print.

Hughes, Langston. "I, Too." *Selected Poems of Langston Hughes.* New York: Vintage Books, 1959. 275. Print.

"Incendiary Pictures." *The Anti-Slavery Record* 2.8 (August 1836): 84. Print.

Jameson, Frederic. *The Political Unconscious: Narrative as a Socially Symbolic Act.* Ithaca: Cornell UP, 1981. Print.

Jentz, John. "The Antislavery Constituency in Jacksonian New York City." *Civil War History* 27.2 (1981): 101–22. Print.

Jones, Robert. "The Hidden Hand: A Drama, in Five Acts. Adapted from Mrs. Emma D.E.N. Southworth's celebrated novel of the same name, published in the New York Ledger." Boston: George M. Baker, 1867. Print.

Karcher, Carolyn. *The First Woman in the Republic: A Cultural Biography of Lydia Maria Child.* Durham: Duke UP, 1994. Print.

Kate [Harriot F. Curtis]. "Aunt Letty; Or, the Useful." *Lowell Offering* Vol. 3. Lowell: William Schouler, 1843. 25–30. Print.

Koven, Seth and Sonya Michel, eds. *Mothers of a New World: Maternalist Politics and the Origins of Welfare States.* New York: Routledge, 1993. Print.

Lapsansky, Philip. "Graphic Discord: Abolitionist and Anti-abolitionist Images," in *The Abolitionist Sisterhood: Women's Political Culture in Ante-bellum America.* Ed. Jean Fagan Yellin, et al. Ithaca: Cornell UP, 1994. 201–30. Print.

Lasch, Christopher. *Haven in a Heartless World.* New York: Basic Books Inc., 1977. Print.

Lauhon, Carol Sinclair Cameron. "Capitola!: Or, Our American Dream: *The Hidden Hand* in American Culture, 1859–1929." Diss. U of Iowa, 2005. Print.

Lebergott, Stanley. *Manpower and Economic Growth: The American Record Since 1800.* New York: McGraw Hill, 1964. Print.

Leopold, Richard William. *Robert Dale Owen: A Biography.* Cambridge: Harvard UP, 1940. Print.

Loggins, Vernon. *The Hawthornes: The Story of Seven Generations of an American Family.* New York: Columbia UP, 1951. Print.

Looby, Christopher. "Southworth and Seriality: *The Hidden Hand* in the *New York Ledger.*" *Nineteenth-Century Literature.* 59.2 (2004): 179–211. Print.

Lowell, Maria. "The Slave-mother." *The Liberty Bell.* Boston: Massachusetts Anti-Slavery Fair, 1846. Print.

Lucinda [Harriet Farley]. "Abby's Year in Lowell." *Lowell Offering* Vol. 1. Lowell: Powers and Bagley, 1841. 1–8. Print.

Lugo, Alejandro and Bill Maurer, eds. *Gender Matters: Rereading Michelle Z. Rosaldo.* Ann Arbor: Michigan UP, 2000. Print.

Magdol, Edward. *The Antislavery Rank and File: A Social Profile of the Abolitionists' Constituency.* New York: Greenwood Press, 1986. Print.

Martin, Waldo E., Jr. *The Mind of Frederick Douglass.* Chapel Hill, University of North Carolina Press, 1984. Print.

Mayer, Henry. *All on Fire: William Lloyd Garrison and the Abolition of Slavery.* New York: St. Martin's Press, 1998. Print.

McFeely, William S. *Frederick Douglass.* New York: W.W. Norton & Co., 1991. Print.

Melville, Herman. "Bartleby, The Scrivener: A Story of Wall-Street." *The Piazza Tales and Other Prose Pieces: 1839–1860.* Chicago: Northwestern UP, 1987. 13–45. Print.

——. "The Paradise of Bachelors and the Tartarus of Maids." *The Piazza Tales and Other Prose Pieces: 1839–1860.* Chicago: Northwestern UP, 1987. 316–35. Print.

A Member of the N.Y. Society for the Abolition of ALL Slavery. "To Feargus O'Connor." *The Working Man's Advocate* 22 June 1844: 2. Print.

Miller, William Lee. *Arguing About Slavery.* New York: Alfred A. Knopf, 1996. Print.

"New England Workingmen's Association." *Voice of Industry* 5 June 1845: 1. Print.

Noble, Marianne. *The Masochistic Pleasures of Sentimental Literature.* Princeton: Princeton UP, 2000. Print.

"Not near So Bad as We Seem." *The New York Ledger* 8 Jan. 1859: 4. Print.

Oakes, James. *Slavery and Freedom: An Interpretation of the Old South.* New York: W.W. Norton, 1990. Print.

Odell, George C. D. *Annals of the New York Stage: 1857–1865.* Vol. 7. New York: Columbia UP, 1931. Print.

Olmsted, Frederick Law. *The Cotton Kingdom*. 1861. Introduction. Arthur M
    Schlesinger, Sr., Ed. Lawrence N. Powell. New York: Random House, 1984.
    Print.
O'Loughlin, James. "Articulating Uncle Tom's Cabin." *New Literary History* 31.1
    (2000): 573–97. Print.
"An Operative." *Voice of Industry* 12 June 1845: 2. Print.
"Our City." *The New York Ledger* 2 July 1859: 2. Print.
Person, Leland S. "The Dark Labyrinth of Mind: Hawthorne, Hester and the
    Ironies of Racial Mothering." *Studies in American Fiction* 29.1 (Spring 2001):
    33 (16). InfoTrac. Web. 29 May 2007.
Phillips, Wendell. "The Philosophy of the Abolition Movement." *Speeches,
    Lectures, and Letters*. New York: Negro Universities Press, 1968. 98–153.
    Print.
"Recruitment of Female Operatives." *Voice of Industry*. (January 2, 1846). Rpt.
    in *Voice of Industry*. Ed. Rajeev Ruparell. University of Massachusetts Lowell
    Libraries. n.d. Web. 28 May 2009.
Reynolds, Larry J. *European Revolutions and the American Literary Renaissance*.
    New Haven: Yale UP, 1988. Print.
Richardson, Gary. "Plays and Playwrights: 1800–1865." *The Cambridge History
    of American Theater*. Ed. Don B. Wilmeth and Christopher Bigsby. New York:
    Cambridge UP, 1998. 250–302. Print.
Roediger, David. "Ira Steward and the Anti-Slavery Origins of American Eight-
    Hour Theory." *Labor History* 27 (1986): 410–26. Print.
———. *The Wages of Whiteness: Race and the Making of the American Working Class*.
    New York: Verso Press, 1991. Print.
Rohrbach, Augusta. *Truth Stranger than Fiction: Race, Realism and the U.S.
    Literary Marketplace*. New York: Palgrave, 2002. Print.
Romero, Lora. *Home Fronts: Domesticity and its Critics in the Antebellum United
    States*. Durham: Duke UP, 1997. Print.
Rothman, David J. *The Discovery of the Asylum: Social Order and Disorder in the
    New Republic*. Rev. ed. New York: Walter de Gruyter, 2002. Print.
Sanchez-Eppler, Karen. "Playing at Class." *ELH* 67 (2000): 819–42. *JSTOR*.
    Web. 12 March 2005.
———. *Touching Liberty: Abolition, Feminism, and the Politics of the Body*. Berkeley:
    University of California Press, 1993. Print.
Seltzer, Mark. *Bodies and Machines*. New York: Routledge, 1992. Print.
Separate Spheres No More: *Gender Convergence in American Literature, 1830–
    1930*. Ed. Monika M. Elbert, Tuscaloosa: U. of Alabama Press, 2000. Print.
Sewall, Samuel. *The Selling of Joseph*. Boston: University of Massachusetts, 1969.
    Print.
Shapiro, Herbert, "Labor and Antislavery: Reflections on the Literature," *Nature,
    Society, and Thought* 2.4 (1989). 471–90. Print.
Siracusa, Carl. *A Mechanical People: Perceptions of the Industrial Order in Mas-
    sachusetts, 1815–1850*. Middletown, CT: Wesleyan UP, 1979.
Sklar, Kathryn Kish. "The Historical Foundations of Women's Power in the Cre-
    ation of the American Welfare State, 1830–1930." *Mothers of a New World:*

Maternalist Politics and the Origins of Welfare States. Ed. Seth Koven and Sonya Michel. New York: Routledge, 1993. Print.

Southworth, E.D.E.N. "The Better Way; Or, the Wife's Victory" *Old Neighborhoods and New Settlements.* New York: A. Hart, 1853. Rpt. in *Uncle Tom's Cabin and American Culture*, Ed. Stephen Railton. University of Virginia. 2007. Web. 8 August 2007.

———. *The Curse of Clifton.* 1852. New York: AMS Press, 1970. Print.

———. *The Hidden Hand or, Capitola the Madcap.* 1859. Ed. Joanne Dobson. New Brunswick: Rutgers UP, 1988. Print.

———. Ishmael; or, in the Depths. 1876. New York: New York Book Co., 1911. Print.

———. "The Married Shrew: A Sequel to "The Better Way." *Old Neighborhoods and New Settlements.* New York: A. Hart, 1853. Rpt. in *Uncle Tom's Cabin and American Culture*, Ed. Stephen Railton. University of Virginia. 2007. Web. 8 August 2007.

———. *Retribution: A Novel.* 1849. Chicago: M.A. Donohue and Company, ca1890. Print.

Stansell, Christine. *City of Women: Sex and Class in New York, 1789–1860.* Chicago, University of Illinois Press, 1982. Print.

Stauffer, John. *The Black Hearts of Men: Radical Abolitionists and the Transformation of Race.* Cambridge: Harvard UP, 2002. Print.

Stewart, Veronica. "Narrative Freedom in E.D.E.N. Southworth's *The Hidden Hand or, Capitola the Madcap.*" LIT 8(1997): 153–72. Print.

Stowe, Harriet Beecher. *A Key to Uncle Tom's Cabin.* 1853. Port Washington, NY: Kennikat Press, 1968. Print.

———. *Uncle Tom's Cabin.* 1852. New York: Penguin Books, 1981. Print.

Subjects & Citizens: Nation, Race, and Gender From Oroonoko to Anita Hill. Ed. Michael Moon and Cathy Davidson. Durham: Duke UP, 1995. Print.

Sumner, Charles. "On the Crime Against Kansas." Senate. 19 May 1856. Speech. Web. 6 September 2007. <http://jefferson.village.virginia.edu/seminar/unit4/sumner.html>.

Sundquist, Eric. Introduction. Ed. Charles Chesnutt. *The Marrow of Tradition.* New York: Penguin Books, 1993. vii-xliv. Print.

Tise, Larry E. *Proslavery: A History of the Defense of Slavery in America, 1701–1840.* Athens: The University of Georgia Press, 1987. Print.

"The Truant Husband." *Voice of Industry* 24 July 1845: 4. Print.

Twain, Mark. *Life on the Mississippi.* 1896. Toronto: Bantam Books, 1981. Print.

Viola. "A Woman's Voice to Woman." *Lowell Offering* (March 1841): 52–53. Print.

"A Week in the Mills." *Lowell Offering.* Vol. 5. Lowell: Misses Curtis and Farley, 1845. 217–18. Print.

Wells-Barnett, Ida B. *On Lynchings: Southern Horrors, A Red Record, Mob Rule in New Orleans.* New York: Arno Press, 1969. Print.

"Who Bids? Incendiary Pictures." *The Anti-Slavery Record* 2.8 (August 1836). Rpt. in *Uncle Tom's Cabin and American Culture.* Ed. Stephen Railton. University of Virginia, 2007. Web. 10 July 2008.

Wilentz, Sean. *Chants Democratic: New York City & the Rise of the American Working Class, 1788–1850*. Oxford: Oxford UP, 1984. Print.

Williams, Raymond. *Marxism and Literature*. Oxford: Oxford UP, 1977. Print.

——. *Problems in Materialism and Culture*. New York: Verso, 1980. Print.

Winthrop, John. "A Modell of Christian Charity." 1630. Boston: Collections of the Massachusetts Historical Society, 1996. *Hanover Historical Texts Project*. Web. 6 June 2007.

Wood, Ellen Meiksins. *Democracy against Capitalism: Renewing Historical Materialism*. Cambridge: Cambridge UP, 1995. Print.

Yazawa, Melvin. *From Colonies to Commonwealth: Familial Ideology and the Beginnings of the American Republic*. Baltimore: Johns Hopkins UP, 1985. Print.

Yellin, Jean Fagan. "Hawthorne and the American National Sin." *The Green American Tradition: Essays and Poems for Sherman Paul*. Ed. Alfred Kazin. Baton Rouge: Louisianna State UP, 1989, 75–97. Print.

——. *Women & Sisters: The Antislavery Feminists and American Culture*. New Haven: Yale UP, 1989. Print.

INDEX